Poetry Today

A Critical Guide to British Poetry
1960–1995

Anthony Thwaite

Longman
London and New York

In association with
The British Council

Longman Group Limited,
Longman House, Burnt Mill,
Harlow, Essex CM20 2JE, England
and Associated Companies throughout the world.

Published in the United States of America
by Longman Publishing, New York

First published 1996

ISBN 0-582-21511-0 PPR

British Library Cataloguing-in-Publication Data
A catalogue record for this book is
available from the British Library

Library of Congress Cataloging-in-Publication Data
Thwaite, Anthony.
    Poetry today: a critical guide to British poetry,
  1960–1995 / Anthony Thwaite.
          p. cm.
    Includes bibliographical references and index.
    ISBN 0-582-21511-0
    1. English poetry—20th century—History and
    criticism.
  I. British Council. II. Title.
PR611.T485   1996
821'.91409—dc20   95–21683
                                                            CIP

Set by 5 in 10/12pt Bembo
Produced by Longman Singapore Publishers (Pte) Ltd.
Printed in Singapore

087619362

821·91409

Contents

List of Illustrations

Prefatory Note

This is the third version, again revised and updated, of a survey
which the British Council commissioned well over twenty
years ago, and which was published as *Poetry Today 1960–1973*.
In 1985 there followed *Poetry Today: A Critical Guide to British
Poetry 1960–1984*. Publication of that version seemed to bring
in its wake the deaths of more poets than looked decent:
Sir John Betjeman, Basil Bunting, W.S. Graham, Robert Graves,
Geoffrey Grigson, Philip Larkin and Stephen Spender. Now,
after ten further years, I have gone over the whole thing again,
trying to take stock, to make many revisions, and to add a large
number of new names.

This time I have attempted to follow a course which
perhaps I should have followed in the earlier versions: that is, if
I have nothing to say about a particular poet, I have not said it.
Most of us have blank areas or blind spots, and these probably
get worse as one grows older. The bibliography contains many
more names and titles than are actually discussed.

Recent years have shown signs of press interest in new
poetry and poets, and there has even been some excitable 'hype'
of a sort last seen in the 1960s. The final section of this survey
tries to put this in the context of 'The Poetry Business'.

Anthony Thwaite   Low Tharston, Norfolk, 1995

Acknowledgements

Thanks are due to the following publishers, authors and literary agents for permission to quote from works in copyright:

Aitken, Stone & Wylie Ltd: 'The Making of a Movement' by Ian Hamilton from *A Poetry Chronicle* (Faber & Faber, 1973).

Anvil Poetry Press Ltd: Carol Ann Duffy 'Making Money' and 'Who Loves You' from *The Other Country* (1990) and 'Prayer' from *Mean Time* (1993).

Bloodaxe Books Ltd: *Out of the Rain* by Glyn Maxwell (1992), *The Bradford Count* by Ian Duhig (1991), *The Way We Live* by Kathleen Jamie (1987), *The Frighteners* by Sean O'Brien (1987).

Edwin Brock: *Five Ways to Kill a Man: New and Selected Poems* (Enitharmon Press, 1990).

Alan Brownjohn: *A Night in the Gazebo* (Secker & Warburg, 1980)

Carcanet Press Ltd: *Collected Poems* by Donald Davie (1990), *Turning the Stones* by Alistair Elliot (1993), *Selected Poetry* by Robert Graves, (1995), *Collected Poems* by P J Kavanagh, (1992), *Collected Poems* by Edwin Morgan (1990), *Collected Poems* by Iain Crichton Smith (1992).

Jonathan Clowes Ltd: Kingsley Amis *A Look Round the Estate*, Copyright © 1967 Kingsley Amis.

J M Dent: *Collected Poems 1945–1990* by R S Thomas (1993).

Dufour Editions Inc, USA: Geoffrey Hill 'Three Baroque Meditations'. 'Funeral Music' and 'From the Latin'.

Gavin Ewart: 'The Death of a Mouse' from *Penultimate Poems* (Hutchinson, 1989)

Faber & Faber Inc, USA: Wendy Cope, *Making Cocoa for Kingsley Amis* and *Serious Concerns*.

Faber & Faber Ltd: Simon Armitage, *Kid* (1992), and *Book of Matches* (1993); W H Auden, *Collected Poems* (1976), edited by Edward Mendelson; Wendy Cope, *Making Cocoa for Kingsley Amis* (1986) and *Serious Concerns* (1992); Douglas Dunn, *Terry Street* (1969). *St Kilda's Parliament* (1981), *Elegies* (1985), and *Dante's Drum Kit* (1993); Thom Gunn, *The Man With Night Sweats* (1992); Seamus Heaney, *Death of a Naturalist* (1966), *Wintering Out* (1972), *North* (1975), and *Seeing Things* (1991); Ted Hughes, *Crow: From Life and Work of the Crow* (1970), *Remains of Elmet* (1979), *Moortown Diary* (1979), and

John Murray (Publishers) Ltd: John Betjeman, *Summoned by Bells* (1976) and *Collected Poems* (1988); George Mackay Brown, *Selected Poems* (1991).

New Directions Publishing Corporation, USA: Stevie Smith, *The Collected Poems of Stevie Smith*.

Oxford University Press: Michael Donaghy, *Shibboleth* (1988) *Errata* (1993); Derek Mahon, *Poems 1962–1978* (1979); Peter Porter, *Collected Poems* (1983); Craig Raine, *A Martian Sends a Postcard Home* (1979); Christopher Reid, *Arcadia* (1979); Peter Scupham, *Watching the Perseids* (1990); George Szirtes, *Selected Poems 1976–1996* (1996).

Oxford University Press, USA: Geoffrey Hill, 'The Laurel Axe' and 'God's Little Mountain'; Robert Graves 'A Dream of Frances Speedwell' and 'Dance of Words'.

Penguin Books Ltd: 'God's Little Mountain', 'Three Baroque Meditations', 'Funeral Music', 'From the Latin', 'Mercian Hymns I', 'Mercian Hymns XXVII', 'The Laurel Axe' from Geoffrey Hill, *Collected Poems* (1985) Copyright © Geoffrey Hill.

Peterloo Poets: U A Fanthorpe, *Side Effects* (1978) Copyright © U A Fanthorpe; John Whitworth, *Tennis and Sex and Death* (1989).

Peters Fraser & Dunlop Ltd: James Fenton, *The Memory of War and Children in Exile* (Penguin, 1983) *Manila Envelope* (James Fenton), *Out of Danger* (Penguin, 1993); John Hegley, *Can I Come Down Now Dad?* (Methuen, 1991 US and South African rights); Michael Longley, *Exploded View* (Gollancz, 1973), *The Echo Gate* (Secker & Warburg, 1979) and *Gorse Fires* (Secker & Warburg, 1991); Blake Morrison, *The Ballad of the Yorkshire Ripper* (Chatto and Windus, 1987), *Dark Glasses* (Chatto and Windus, 1984); Andrew Motion, *Love in a Life* (Faber & Faber, 1991 US rights).

Random House Inc, USA: W H Auden, *Collected Poems*.

Random House UK Ltd: Norman MacCaig, *Collected Poems* (Chatto and Windus, 1993); The Estate of William Plomer, *Taste and Remember* (Cape, 1966).

Peter Reading: *Ukulele Music*, (Secker & Warburg, 1985).

Reed Books: Alan Brownjohn, *In the Cruel Arcade* (Sinclair-Stevenson, 1994); Geoffrey Grigson, *Persephone's Flowers and Other Poems* (Secker & Warburg, 1986); John Hegley, *Can I Come Down Now Dad?* (Methuen, 1991); Michael Longley, *Gorse Fires* (Secker & Warburg, 1991); George Macbeth, *Poems from Oby*, (Secker & Warburg, 1982); John Mole, *Homing* (Secker & Warburg, 1987); George Szirtes, *The Slant Door*, (Secker & Warburg, 1979).

1

Poetry today: the place of the anthology

Throughout the present century, the programmatic and polemical anthology has been one of the most conspicuous instruments of change, or attempted change. As long ago as 1920, Harold Monro (founder of the Poetry Bookshop) saw this, as he surveyed successive volumes of *Georgian Poetry*, the Imagist anthologies, Ezra Pound's *Catholic Anthology*, *Wheels* (chiefly a display-case for the Sitwell family and its associates), and even the retrograde *Poems of To-day*, which sold in its tens of thousands, not as a revolutionary collection but as a safe and comforting textbook for use in schools. As Monro acidly remarked, 'The book created no sensation: it has been an amazing success'.

The past sixty years have seen a number of anthologies which attempted to be – and in a few cases actually became – key literary documents of their time. In *New Signatures* (1932) and *New Country* (1933) Michael Roberts presented the young W.H. Auden, Stephen Spender, C. Day Lewis and William Empson as the new poets; and soon after, in his important *Faber Book of Modern Verse* (1936), Roberts set these poets (together with more recent arrivals, such as Dylan Thomas, George Barker and David Gascoyne) in the context of the whole century, beginning with Gerard Manley Hopkins (who, though he died in 1889, was not properly published until 1918). Roberts' Introduction to this anthology is still well worth reading as a very intelligent undoctrinaire essay on what later acquired the academic/historical label 'Modernism'.

Roberts' emphasis in the 1930s could be seen, not wholly inaccurately, as political and social. In the early years of the Second World War, the anthology *The White Horseman* (1941), appeared to represent and stress a different emphasis. As the flagship of the neo-romantic 'New Apocalypse', it set out to 'mount guard over the integrity of the imagination and the completeness of man', with gesturings towards Herbert Read,

Stephen Spender
Caroline Forbes

Jung, Dylan Thomas; but the book's aspirations were belied by
its largely feeble and incoherent contents.

Ten years after the end of the war, the poets of the so-called
'Movement' had emerged. In 1956, Robert Conquest's *New
Lines* tried to show that 'a genuine and healthy poetry of the
new period has established itself'; and the exemplary figures
were Kingsley Amis, Donald Davie, D.J. Enright, Thom Gunn,
Philip Larkin. But to some this was mere revisionism, too tame
and too parochial. A. Alvarez's *The New Poetry* (1962, revised
edition 1965) carried a preface which was a call for 'a new
seriousness', defined as 'the poet's ability and willingness to
face the full range of his experience with his full intelligence',
without taking the easy exits of 'the conventional response or
choking incoherence', and eschewing what Alvarez saw as the
deadly English condition, 'gentility'. In this, the confessional
Americans John Berryman and Robert Lowell (and, after her

death in 1963, Sylvia Plath) were presented as exemplary, and Ted Hughes's 'violent, impending presence' was contrasted with Larkin's supposed genteel nostalgias.

'Urgency' was one of Alvarez's touchstones; but twenty years later, when Blake Morrison and Andrew Motion edited *The Penguin Book of Contemporary British Poetry*, this was regarded with scorn, and *The New Poetry* itself as 'a historical document'. The new exemplary figures, all prominently represented by Morrison and Motion, were Seamus Heaney, Tony Harrison, Douglas Dunn, James Fenton, Craig Raine and Christopher Reid. Larkin, reviewing the anthology, asked:

> But where is the message? If Conquest was for common sense, and Alvarez anti-genteel, what are Morrison/Motion advocating? Hard to say.

And Larkin went on to quote from the Morrison/Motion Introduction:

> They have developed a degree of ludic and literary self-consciousness reminiscent of the modernists . . . It manifests, in other words, a preoccupation with relativism . . . The new poetry is often open-ended, reluctant to point the moral of, or conclude too neatly, what it chooses to transcribe.

'Not easy to make a slogan out of that', Larkin dryly commented.

Yet *The Penguin Book of Contemporary British Poetry* at its appearance in 1982 did indeed turn out to be controversial, in spite of what Larkin saw as its lack of a clarion 'message'. Although it copiously represented Northern Irish poets (not only Heaney but Michael Longley, Derek Mahon, Tom Paulin, Paul Muldoon, Medbh McGuckian), and gave a good deal of prominence to such unmetropolitans as Douglas Dunn and Tony Harrison, it was seen in unfriendly quarters to be tainted by 'metropolitan' values. Morrison and Motion have held, and hold, important positions as literary middlemen (variously, on *The Times Literary Supplement*, *The Observer*, *Poetry Review*, more recently on *The Independent on Sunday* and in London publishing houses). Such provincial outposts as Manchester (home of the Carcanet Press and *P.N. Review*) and Newcastle (Bloodaxe Books) smelt conspiracy, London networks, 'elitism', in these supposed allegiances.

Every generation of poets wants to follow Pound's injunction 'make it new' – or, if they don't, there will be organisers there who urge them to do so, fielding teams and squads which are presented not only as exemplary but as *salons des réfusés*. So, in 1993, the three editors of *The New Poetry* (Michael Hulse, David Kennedy and David Morley), published by Bloodaxe, set out their own stall: 'what we believe to be the best poetry written in the British Isles in the 1980s and early 1990s by a distinctive new generation of poets'.

They created a self-imposed exclusion zone: they would not include anyone represented in the Morrison/Motion anthology, or anyone born before 1940. They also began their Introduction with the dubious opinion: 'Every age gets the literature it deserves', and went on with other opinions and phrases which were probably calculated to annoy. However, the central slogan seems to be no more exciting or inflammatory than anything in the Penguin Book: 'plurality has replaced monocentric totemism'.

As usual, the poets included seem less radically different from all that had gone before than the polemics suggest; nor can they be seen as struggling outsiders. By the time *The New Poetry* was published in 1993, one of the book's central presences, Peter Reading, had published fifteen books, beginning in 1974, and he had won several of the main poetry awards. Not only that, but all except one of his books had been published by mainstream commercial London publishers. Other poets included, though less conspicuously represented, could be seen as 'metropolitan' (or 'Oxbridge' – another mark of the beast) in their publishers or in the way they earned their livings: David Constantine, Bernard O'Donoughue (Oxford dons); Kit Wright, Selima Hill, George Szirtes, Sean O'Brien, Michael Donaghy, Michael Hofmann, Simon Armitage – all of them published by such 'establishment' firms as Hutchinson, Chatto & Windus, Oxford University Press, and Faber. An artificial dichotomy thrust between provincial/metropolitan (or North/South) looks opportunist rather than principled.

Even the anthology's insistence on making central those whose work had been 'marginalised' (through being women, or immigrants, as well as by being provincial) looks like a doubtful, indeed false, strategy. The most impressive woman poet in the book is Carol Ann Duffy, who from the beginning of her career in the early 1980s has never seemed in danger of being on the margin of anything. True, she has until recently stayed loyally with the small press (Anvil – actually a London firm) that published her first book in 1985; but this clearly hasn't prevented her from winning awards, prizes and fellowships, or from becoming one of the most widely travelled (and best paid) readers on the circuits.

The immigrants – or, more properly, those of immigrant background, since most of them are long-time British residents, if not actually born in Britain – include Grace Nichols, Linton Kwesi Johnson, David Dabydeen, Sujata Bhatt, Fred D'Aguiar, and Jackie Kay. Of these six contributors to *The New Poetry*, only Johnson can sensibly be seen as a conscious outsider, someone who uses pretty consistently his own transcribed idiom (more a matter of orthography than anything else) to insist his own separateness.

If it comes to that, one might make a case – though it wouldn't be one I would press – for the self-conscious separateness of some Irish and Scottish poets. Paul Durcan, the most extraordinary talent to have come out of the Irish Republic for many years, needs no such gingerly treatment; but Nuala Ní Dhomhnaill is the solitary writer in *The New Poetry* who uses a totally foreign language – her three poems are in Irish, and those unskilled in the language have to rely on accompanying English versions by Paul Muldoon and Seamus Heaney (otherwise kept out of the anthology by the editors' exclusions, mentioned earlier). One wonders what accommodation the editors made for any Welsh-writing candidates. Further, W.N. Herbert has three poems which are entertainingly written in something one used to call Lallans – the Scottish literary/demotic grafted on to something which is just recognisably English.

All this vaunting attempt at 'plurality' perhaps seems to support the case that the editors of *The New Poetry* appear to be making about poetry in Britain in the early 1990s. Certainly their fifty-five poets range across a wide spectrum. But the opposition – 'monocentric totemism' – seems no more than a convenient bogey-figure, yet another way of characterising the endless story of the past being obliterated to yield to the new. Perhaps, indeed, it is simply a brash and unconvincing manner of saying what Jonathan Swift put more incisively and wittily about two and a half centuries ago:

> Every poet in his kind
> Is bit by him who comes behind.

2

Robert Graves and David Jones

In the gloomy roll-call of poets who died in 1985, the oldest was Robert Graves, aged ninety. For ten years he had been poetically silent, but until then he was writing and publishing poems of a sharpness, tenderness, or quizzical waywardness as fresh as many he had written years earlier. Graves was almost the last link with the survivors of the First World War, and also someone who was a slightly younger contemporary of the great Modernists (T.S. Eliot, Ezra Pound) without being a Modernist himself. Many of Graves's later poems are stylish, subdued, deeply romantic in feeling but classically laconic in expression, with a courtliness of address which became his characteristic tone. In 'Dance of Words'*, for example:

> To make them move, you should start from lightning
> And not forecast the rhythm: rely on chance,
> Or so-called chance for its bright emergency
> Once lightning interpenetrates the dance.
>
> Grant them their own traditional steps and postures
> But see they dance it out again and again
> Until only lightning is left to puzzle over –
> The choreography plain, and the theme plain.

Many of Graves's later poems were love poems, in which the object often seemed to be an amalgam of a younger woman adored by an old man, the 'immanent Goddess' or muse to

*Most of the quotations from poems reproduced in this survey are extracts. Unabridged poems are indicated by an asterisk.

whom he long professed allegiance, and a figure or figures out of distant but still passionate memory. The last is most prominent in 'A Dream of Frances Speedwell'*, but elements of all three are present:

I fell in love at my first evening party.
You were tall and fair, just seventeen perhaps,
Talking to my two sisters. I kept silent,
And never since have loved a tall fair girl
Until last night in the small windy hours
When, floating up an unfamiliar staircase
And into someone's bedroom, there I found her
Posted beside the window in half-light
Wearing that same white dress with lacy sleeves.
She beckoned. I came closer. We embraced
Inseparably until the dream faded.
Her eyes shone clear and blue . . .

Who was it, though, impersonated you?

These are only two fairly late examples of Graves's skill: he was a prolific poet throughout his long life, and one who restlessly discarded almost as much as he accumulated. His last large-scale assemblage, *Collected Poems 1975*, is generous, but it also needs to be seen against many earlier volumes. For years, his copious production provided no startling shocks or disconcerting shifts, but everything was aimed towards a total unified body of work, exemplified in the fact that each individual volume has been divided into parts numbered as supplements to each successive *Collected Poems*. When a volume – or series of volumes – of *Complete Poems* is eventually published, it is likely to show an intentness of concern remarkable for variety within unity. The contention that Graves was not only prolific but repetitive is a serious one, yet it must accept or reject Graves's own contention that to the poet there is only 'one story'. If it accepts it, it must accept what seems to be repetitiveness too; if rejected, it must look elsewhere for reasons with which to account for the distinctiveness of Robert Graves's contribution to the poetry of the century.

A much more enigmatic member of this pre-1900 generation – those who were already adults at the time of the First World War – was David Jones, poet, painter and graphic artist, whose literary work and personality were as individual as those of Graves but who has attracted a cult-following rather than general affection and admiration. Jones was a 'difficult' writer in a way that Graves never is. Whereas Graves's interest in history, mythology and religion usually expressed itself in prose auxiliary to his verse (of a learned, capriciously scholarly, frequently polemical sort), Jones's involvement with the same subjects went directly into his creative work – *In Parenthesis*, *The Anathemata*, more recently *The Tribune's Visitation* and other more fragmentary pieces. The excitement to be gained from David Jones is of a kind that comes from a strange hinterland where eccentric scholarship, exalted code-cracking and the visionary gleam meet and merge. The setting of many of his later fragments is Palestine in the first century AD. The 'characters' are Roman soldiers, but – as was true of the Roman army itself – these include Celts and Greeks as well as native Romans. Thus a great deal of Celtic and Greek mythology underlies the highly allusive texture of the work, together with those incidents and phrases from modern war and soldiering which were such an integral part of *In Parenthesis*.

There are many contrasts in David Jones's poetry – between innocence and experience, between archaism and modernism, between a tenuous romantic mysticism and a hard precision of language. Underneath them all lies a preoccupation with the continuity of the Christian faith, seen in different guises and in different perspectives, sometimes underlying primitive ritual, sometimes shadowed in the Arthurian legends, often approached through its central mystery of the Mass:

> for all are members
> of the Strider's body.
> And if not of one hope
> then of one necessity.

For we all are attested to one calling
not any more several, but one.
And one to what purpose?
                    and by what necessity?

See! I break this barrack bread, I drink with you, this
issue cup, I salute, with you, these mutilated signa,
I with you have cried with all of us the ratifying
formula: *Idem in me*!
                    So, if the same oath serve
why, let the same illusions fall away.

                                        (*The Tribune's Visitation*)

In a sense, Jones seems to have attempted an historical Christian
counterpart to what Ezra Pound failed to achieve, in my
opinion, in the *Cantos* – a view of the flood of the past and
the way in which it forces itself into the dry channels of the
present. Jones's conviction of a divine transfiguring unifies his
fragments in a way impossible to Pound's secular notions of
'good government'. The achievement is puzzling and not always
apparently coherent, but it is an impressive achievement all the
same.

3

John Betjeman and William Plomer

John Betjeman's tenure as Poet Laureate, from towards the end of 1972 until his death in 1984, was generally acknowledged to have been the most successful in this quaint and archaic office since that of Tennyson. For many years, from his first emergence in the 1930s, he had a cult reputation; but his *Collected Poems*, published in 1958, had a huge and immediate success, selling in its tens of thousands, and the book went on being revised and added to.

Betjeman's popularity is not difficult to account for, but it is certainly difficult to analyse. When he was appointed Laureate, the news was greeted in some quarters with the sort of good–hearted but amused condescension that one imagines might have met the announcement that Dickens' Cheeryble brothers had been invited to join the Cabinet. Betjeman's own presentation of himself, on television and in interviews, as a bumbling, untidy, genial, cranky, harmless old buffer had a great deal to do with this, and also the fact that his public preoccupations seemed to have narrowed down to antiquarian preservationism and the championing of Victorian verse. In addition, there was the fact that his best known poems, such as 'A Subaltern's Love-song' ('Miss Joan Hunter Dunn, Miss Joan Hunter Dunn'), are gently absurd essays in light verse.

But there is an altogether more astringent side to Betjeman, in which nostalgia, fear, terror, hard-won faith and simple goodness contend, and a feline ferocity which is sometimes startling. The easy surfaces, lyrical measures or ambling pedestrianism of his poetry move about areas of experience which are not simple at all, and which had no proper voice until he gave them one: as much as Eliot, he created the taste by which he is enjoyed. Of course he was not an innovatory and influential figure on the scale of Eliot, but his short-range colonising of traditional areas – his awareness of the Tradition, in fact – can be seen as quite as original and striking as Eliot's grander imperialism.

Summoned by Bells (1960), the verse autobiography which took him from childhood to going down dimly and regretfully from Oxford, was his most sustained effort, though he published many attractive shorter poems after it. Written mainly in correct but conversational blank verse, interspersed with the hymn-like rhyming stanzas he often used elsewhere, *Summoned by Bells* is full of what Betjeman himself called 'rapid changes of mood and subject', so that it comprehends a whole complex growing personality, lightly, gravely, accurately:

> Atlantic rollers bursting in my ears,
> And pealing church-bells and the puff of trains,
> The sight of sailing clouds, the smell of grass –
> Were always calling out to me for words.
> I caught at them and missed and missed again.
> 'Catch hold', my father said, 'catch hold like this!',
> Trying to teach me how to carpenter,
> 'Not *that* way boy! When will you ever learn?' –
> I dug the chisel deep into my hand.
> 'Shoot!' said my father, helping with my gun
> And aiming at the rabbit – 'Quick, boy, fire!'
> But I had not released the safety-catch.
> I was a poet. That was why I failed.
> My faith in this chimera brought an end
> To all my father's hopes. In later years,
> Now old and ill, he asked me once again
> To carry on the firm, I still refused.
> And now when I behold, fresh-published, new,
> A further volume of my verse, I see
> His kind grey eyes look woundedly at mine,
> I see his workmen seeking other jobs,
> And that red granite obelisk that marks
> The family grave in Highgate Cemetery
> Points an accusing finger to the sky.

In a broadcast critical survey of his reputation, transmitted a year after his death, a variety of poets praised him and tried to pin down the qualities of his originality and his skills. Philip Larkin thought he would survive 'as a poet of great energy. Once you begin reading a poem by Betjeman you immediately feel you're in good hands; he's not going to let you down.' But Larkin also commented that Betjeman seemed to him 'more a dark poet than a light poet – a great obsession with death. The first poem in the first book he published – "Death in Leamington" – it epitomises Betjeman: death on the one hand, the precise place on the other.' It seems that his work by no means appeals exclusively to the 'upper-middle-class and lower-middle-aged' public characterised as such by a derogatory commentator – though, in the broadcast survey, Tom Paulin spoke of him as representing 'that anti-intellectual antiquarian streak that there is in English culture . . . that kind of whimsy which, after a while, becomes terrible and frightening and surreal and bizarre, because of its enormous, trivialising stupidity'.

One can perhaps understand such a reaction, without endorsing it, when reading a phrase used of him at his death – that (according to *The Times*) he had become a 'teddy bear to the nation'. Some of his admirers have been corrupted by cosiness – but that is not Betjeman's fault. Auden praised him for his versatile technical skill, Larkin praised him not only for his energy but for his 'dramatic urgency' that springs from 'what he really feels about real life'. The urgency is part of the skill, speaking nakedly but with decorum from a basic melancholy, as in 'NW5 and N6'. In this poem, the careful and circumstantial re-creation of childhood, of a sadistic nurse imposing her puritan will in the midst of outwardly cosy suburbia, moves to its blank and bleak conclusion:

'World without end'. It was not what she'ld do
That frightened me so much as did her fear
And guilt at endlessness. I caught them too,
Hating to think of sphere succeeding sphere
Into eternity and God's dread will
I caught her terror then. I have it still.

William Plomer was often paired with John Betjeman, and it is true that both emerged in the early 1930s as satirists and writers of light verse. Plomer went on to develop his own brand of 'sick' humour, most outrageously and memorably in such poems of the 1940s as 'The Dorking Thigh', 'The Flying Bum' and 'The Self-Made Blonde'. All these are exercises in straight-faced shock, and the urbane mockery rides easily over the gruesome nastiness of the incidents described. In them, Plomer toyed elegantly with the bizarre, using brisk and breezy stanzas and jaunty rhymes. In his later work there was much less concern with satire and absurdity. Pathos and wistfulness seemed to have taken over, in such poems as 'Lime-Flower Tea', in which an old man walks the esplanade of a seaside town before returning to his 'neurotic childless wife':

> His walk alone at night she understands
> And the unsaid;
> In the warm room she'll pour out,
> Before bed,
> Delicately, lime-flower tea;
> Together they will sip and dream,
> Sad and content, both drugged
> By the lost summer in the scented steam.

This is one of the fragile successes of *Taste and Remember*, the volume from which it comes; but it is a mark of one's old expectations that at a first reading the poem seems to be poised for some horrific conclusion – the man killing his wife with arsenic in that lime-flower tea, or strangling her with his old school tie. The thought is unworthy, but it is difficult to escape the conviction that the gravity, thoughtfulness and sincerity of Plomer's later poems have a heaviness of language and movement which, together with an emotional obviousness, lack the distinction of his former shockers.

4

W.H. Auden, Louis MacNeice, C. Day Lewis, Stephen Spender

The old quadrumvirate of the 1930s, lampooned into mythical unity by Roy Campbell as 'MacSpaunday', has long since disintegrated. Auden continues to be the commanding figure, long after his death in 1973, and his assiduous literary executor, Edward Mendelson, continues to produce comprehensive editions of his works – poetry, drama, libretti, criticism. Louis MacNeice died in 1963, C. Day Lewis in 1972. The last survivor was Stephen Spender who died in 1995. His *Collected Poems 1928–85* was highly selective. It left out a great deal, and much of what it included often turned out to be rewritten, so that familiar poems were sometimes defamiliarised, not always to their advantage. But in 1994 he produced a new volume, *Dolphins*, on his 85th birthday: his sheer lively survival, together with his importance as 'man of letters' for over sixty years, made Spender an almost talismanic figure.

There are some who hold to a persuasion (loyal but aggrieved, given to disappointment rather than condemnation) that W.H. Auden's importance as a poet began to diminish rapidly and disastrously with his departure to America not long before the Second World War. Such people instance prolixity where there used to be terseness, smugness where there was unease, cosy verbal games in place of urgent and memorable warnings. But the decade of the 1930s – in the English-speaking world of poetry so much the Age of Auden – is not a period to be prolonged out of feelings of nostalgia, whether genuine or vicarious; the *Poems* (1930) still survive, and *The Orators*, and all the rest of the pre-1941 work, whatever Auden did or didn't do to it in the way of revision or suppression. It is an assembly of work that embodies a period in the way that much good poetry does, but we should not expect Auden in his sixties to perpetuate – by imitation, as it were – the Auden of his twenties and thirties. He became a sage rather than a prophet; but above all he was still supremely an entertainer, a virtuoso who believed that poetry can display many voices, many skills, and that it has something to do with the disinterested intelligence:

> After all, it's rather a privilege
>   amid the affluent traffic
> to serve this unpopular art which cannot be turned into
>   background noise for study
> or hung as a status trophy by rising executives,
>   cannot be 'done' like Venice
> or abridged like Tolstoy, but stubbornly still insists upon
>   being read or ignored: our handful
> of clients at least can rune.

('The Cave of Making')

I think it is worth noting that younger poets (such as John Fuller and James Fenton) who have responded sympathetically and affectionately to Auden during these past few years have done so with particular attention to the post-war poetry – *Nones, Homage to Clio, About the House,* and so on. Auden is still a force, not a spent one.

About the House (1966) is the first of the Auden books to fall within the period of this essay, and it had three serious successors, *City Without Walls* (1969), *Epistle to a Godson* (1972) and *Thank You, Fog* (1974): *Academic Graffiti* (1971) can be bracketed off as the entertainer indulging himself with games that could be properly characterised as cosy, unashamedly minor, and often not very successful even on their own terms. The Auden of the other books is someone who gratefully found a way of life and a place in which to live it: the twelve poems in 'Thanksgiving for a Habitat' (from *About the House*) in particular celebrated his 'toft-and-croft' in Austria, a haven of routine and mild pleasure among his 'own little Anglo-American musico-literary set'. Tetchily content, unconvinced and repelled by the cant of the young and the politically zealous, he frequently looked back to his childhood (a privileged one of nannies and Greek, antique symbols now) and contrasted it with the uncomely present of

> lasers, electric brains,
> do-it-yourself sex manuals,
> bugged phones, sophisticated
> weapon-systems and sick jokes.

('Prologue at Sixty')

Privacy and common sense, friendship and good manners, the blessing of survival itself – these are the daily benefits for which he was thankful. But this *otium liberale*, this cultured retirement, is given its special edge through Auden's peculiar technical gifts, by which the commonplace is enjoyed in a thoroughly uncommonplace vocabulary, erudite, quirky, and often donnishly eccentric:

> In his dream zealous
> To attain his home,
> But ensorcelling powers
> Have contorted space,
> Odded the way:
> Instead of a facile
> Five-minute trot,
> Far he must hirple,
> Clumsied by cold,
> Buffeted often
> By blouts of hail
> Or pirries of rain,
> On stolchy paths
> Over glunch clouds,
> Where infrequent shepherds,

Sloomy of face,
Snudge of spirit,
Snoachy of speech,
With scaddle dogs
Tend a few scrawny
Cag-mag sheep.

('A Bad Night')

He could be grander and less neologistic than this: 'An Encounter' (which observes a meeting between 'Attila and his Hun Horde' and Pope Leo by the River Po in the year 452) needs no recourse to the *Oxford English Dictionary* and makes a real point about the mysteries of civilisation and barbarism. He could also be delightfully straightforward and witty, as in 'On the Circuit', which considers the modern ordeal-by-culture of the peripatetic poet on a reading tour:

An airborne instrument I sit,
Predestined nightly to fulfil
Colombia-Giesen-Management's
Unfathomable will,

[. . .]

And daily, seven days a week,
Before a local sense has jelled,
From talking-site to talking-site
Am jet-or-prop-propelled.

Emotional urgency and a deeply committed sense of struggle both with life and with one's material seem to be basic requirements demanded by many critics of poetry today. The fact that Auden's post-war work conspicuously lacks these, is indeed contemptuous of them, partly accounts for the way in which he has been taken at his own valuation, as a reactionary and rather supercilious mandarin who looked back to a time when

. . . Speech was mannerly, an Art,
Like learning not to belch or fart:
I cannot settle which is worse,
The Anti-Novel or Free Verse.

('Doggerel by a Senior Citizen')

Yet Auden's actual performance, his wide-ranging and individual
experience, equally at home or not-at-home on his 'Austrian
ground', as a carpet-slippered celebrator of Oxford eccentricities
or as 'a New Yorker, who opens his *Times* at the obit page',
belie the limitations he seems to have assigned to himself and
which others have chosen to accept or condemn. 'The Cave of
Making' (his memorial poem for Louis MacNeice), 'Whitsunday
in Kirchstetten', 'Prologue at Sixty', 'Old People's Home',
and 'Talking to Myself' are all poems in which Auden is at
the centre, ruminating, conversational, at ease with himself
but without self-satisfaction, and they speak from true and
deeply-felt concerns with a wisdom and decent mannerliness,
aware without huffing and puffing that

Virtue is always
more expensive than Vice, but
cheaper than Madness

('Shorts II')★

The Auden whose dramatic characters in the 1930s (according
to Isherwood) were always ready to flop on their knees became
less inclined to preach and prescribe, lecture and warn, and
was 'Most at home with what is Real'. His later work had a
different, not an inferior, validity.

When Louis MacNeice died in September 1963, he was
going through a rich and extended creative phase, the evidence
of which can be seen in his last two books, *Solstices* (1961) and
The Burning Perch, which he had prepared for press and which

appeared only a few days after his death. MacNeice had always been a prolific poet, but there had been periods in his life – particularly during the late 1940s and most of the 1950s – when the machine appeared to be running with not much more than fluency: his actual power had seemed to be waning in such work as *Autumn Sequel*, for example. But the last two books are a fine (and, as it turned out, final) flowering, and they contain poems as good as anything he wrote.

MacNeice has increasingly seemed to me the most immediately attractive of the MacSpaunday quartet, and at the same time a much more serious and complex figure than he has sometimes been taken to be. His upbringing as the son of a gloomy Ulster Protestant clergyman ('Between a smoking fire and a tolling bell'), his training as a classical scholar, his quiet relish of the ordinary pleasures of life tempered by a steady and stoical pessimism – all these are elements in his work, and all of them were handled with a well-judged lyrical virtuosity. More and more, a melancholy tunefulness seems the manner of his last poems:

O never force the pace, they said;
Leave it alone, you have lots of time,
Your kind of work is none the worse
For slow maturing. Do not rush.
　　He took their tip, he took his time,
　　And found his time and talent gone.

Oh you have had your chance, It said;
Left it alone and it was one.
Who said a watched clock never moves?
Look at it now. Your chance was I.
　　He turned and saw the accusing clock
　　Race like a torrent round a rock.

('The Slow Starter')

They are not in any ordinary sense the poems of a dying man, for MacNeice's death was sudden and unexpected; yet they are indeed much concerned with slow decline, extinction and nullity, watched with a jaunty and devil-may-care insouciance. Even the games he so enjoyed and celebrated in his poems serve as a text (in 'Sports Page') for the conclusion that

> The lines of print are always sidelines
> And all our games funeral games.

Themes of childhood, of nostalgia, are wedded to forms and metres that often have something of the nursery rhyme or the folk poem about them, and in 'Château Jackson' he builds a whole mysteriously nihilistic *tour de force* on the structure of the old verses about the house that Jack built. The idea of play is strong in MacNeice's last poems, but it is always play with a purpose and done to strict rules: this too is part of the child-world, as is the emphasis on magic, the irrational and dreams, the sense of *déjà vu* which is both exhilarating and frightening:

> It does not come round in hundreds of thousands of years,
> It comes round in the split of a wink, you will be sitting exactly
>
> Where you are now and scratching your elbow, the train
> Will be passing exactly as now and saying It does not come round,
> It does not come round, It does not come round, and compactly
> The wheels will mark time on the rails and the bird in the air
> Sit tight in its box and the same bean of coffee be ground
> That is now in the mill and I know what you're going to say
> For all this has happened before, we both have been through the mill,
>
> ('Déjà vu')

MacNeice's *Collected Poems*, carefully edited by E.R. Dodds and published in 1966, span a period of almost forty years and make up a very varied and substantial body of work. His poems have always been great favourites with the anthologists (I am thinking of such familiar pieces as 'Bagpipe Music', 'The Sunlight on the Garden', 'Prayer Before Birth' and 'Snow'), and there are several in his last two books which will I am sure go on having that sort of life: 'Soap Suds', 'Apple Blossom', 'The Truisms', and – one of the poems written at the very end of his life – 'Thalassa'. But he deserves to be read as a whole, and the *Collected Poems* make up one of the most continuously entertaining books to be published for many years.

C. Day Lewis, who died in 1972 after a long illness, was probably as prolific a writer as MacNeice, and his reputation went through as many fluctuations. After his *Collected Poems* of 1954, he published four further volumes. Many of the poems in them have a sense of being 'occasional' pieces, celebrating dead friends and dead artists, rediscovering places and roots in his native Ireland, commemorating specific moments of pleasure or pain. The manner is sweetly lyrical, gently melancholy, and the general impression is a little too bland. Throughout his poetic career, Day Lewis's chief disablement was that he seemed to respond too easily to the seductive voices of those poets he admired: Auden in his early days, and later a whole *mélange* of influences – in particular Meredith and, most of all, Hardy. His generous and genial temperament tended to soften his mentors, making them diffuse and losing their defining edges. Even such an attractive poem as 'Walking Away' (from *The Gate*, 1962) suffers from this blurring effect: in it, the poet remembers watching his young son, now a grown man, walking away from him to school 'With the pathos of a half-fledged thing set free/Into a wilderness', and the feel of the detail in these first three stanzas is Hardyesque, as is the movement of the verse. But the final stanza moralises in a wistful way that sounds like diluted Robert Frost:

I have had worse partings, but none that so
Gnaws at my mind still. Perhaps it is roughly
Saying what God alone could perfectly show –

How selfhood begins with a walking away,
And love is proved in the letting go.

The sincerity is moving, but it lacks final authenticity because of the echoes, the uneasy awareness of high pastiche.

I think these are proper objections, not mere fussing about 'influences'. Yet the fact remains that Day Lewis's poems give a good deal of pleasure to a large number of people, who perhaps find that emotional honesty and emotional simplicity of his kind, matched with graceful and rather obviously musical cadences, override more rigorous demands. The decent commonplaces of such a poem as 'The House where I was Born' illustrate this well:

No one is left alive to tell me
In which of those rooms I was born,
Or what my mother could see, looking out one April
Morning, her agony done,
Or if there were pigeons to answer my cooings
From that tree to the left of the lawn.

The appearance of Day Lewis's *The Complete Poems* in 1992, comprehensively and self-effacingly edited by his widow, Jill Balcon, gave an opportunity to look at his work more clearly, and perhaps more generously. For myself, I find I still hold to the limiting judgements I have made; but I also find that, read in bulk, *The Complete Poems* show a devotion and a variety, as well as a professionalism, which should help to keep alive an appreciation of Day Lewis's gifts.

The conventional judgement on Stephen Spender's work is that his early poems, in his first two books, are his best. In my opinion it is also the right judgement, and neither the *Collected Poems 1928–85* (selective and often rewritten, as I have said) nor its single successor, *Dolphins* (1994), seem to countermand it. I am not thinking of such early pieces as 'I think continually of those who were truly great' or 'The Express' or 'Landscape

Near an Aerodrome', all of which are familiar anthology entries, but of stumblingly eloquent and strange poems like 'Without that once clear aim', 'Not palaces, an era's crown', 'Two Armies' and 'Port Bou', in which cloudy but passionate states of mind are fixed and defined with sensitive strokes. After that, there seems a gradual loss of verbal conviction; the personality seems much the same, but it has lost its lonely concentration.

This mention of 'personality' needs to be supported. The struggle in Spender had always been between the public man, the man of letters, the *conférencier*, and someone altogether more private, personal, self-absorbed. Many years ago (in 1951), in *World Within World*, that prose memoir which still seduces, charms, and shocks, Spender wrote of himself as 'an autobiographer restlessly searching for forms in which to express the stages of my development'. Poetry, fiction, plays, essays, copious journals – all these have shown a craving for introspection. The nineteen poems in his *Dolphins* confirm this, in their brief compass taking in much of Spender's long lifetime of experience. If they lack – as I believe they do – the strangely luminous authority of Spender's best early poems, at the same time they interestingly and sometimes poignantly illuminate his life. 'A First War Childhood' and 'Worldsworth' go back to 1916 and early memories of the Norfolk coast. The sequence of ten short poems, 'Poètes Maudits', though ostensibly 'about' Verlaine and Rimbaud, is surely to some extent a set of variations or meditations on the life of the poet, self-regarding as well as ventriloquial. Technically, these poems are as oddly casual as Spender's have often been: informal even when highly charged, tending towards the condition of notebook jottings. And the book begins and ends with more lyrically exalted pieces, 'Dolphins' and 'The Alphabet Tree', poems which seem to be ecstatic struggles between Spender's intensely recognised egotism and the last enemy, death. They have a courageous self-consciousness, dissolving themselves in vision.

5

George Barker, David Gascoyne, W.S. Graham, Lawrence Durrell, Norman Nicholson

When he died in 1991, George Barker was noticed in several obituaries as 'the last Romantic' – or at any rate the last of the Bohemians. He was always a problematical figure. He emerged almost as a boy prodigy. With no advantages except his own talent and wayward charm, he published his first book at the age of twenty (*Thirty Preliminary Poems*, 1933), a novel that same year, and in 1935 both a book of poems and a work of prose fiction with T.S. Eliot at Faber. In 1936, when W.B. Yeats published the *Oxford Book of Modern Verse*, Barker was the youngest poet whom Yeats included: 'a lovely subtle mind', wrote Yeats, 'and a rhythmical invention comparable to Gerard Hopkins'.

His career throughout the 1930s was indeed charmed, and for several years Barker was seen as one of the most important poets of the generation that immediately succeeded Auden and MacNeice. But by the time of Dylan Thomas's death in 1953, interest in Barker seemed to have lapsed, in spite of his copious output. In the following years, Barker seemed to be judged as if he lay in the shadow of Thomas's fame. Even the noise over his *True Confession of George Barker* (the first part of which, published in 1950, caused questions about obscenity to be asked in Parliament) faded into silence and neglect.

Though he went on publishing prolifically throughout the 1950s into the 1980s, it was not until the appearance of his long meditative poem *Anno Domini* in 1983, the year of his seventieth birthday, that at last there seemed to be a renewal of interest: Barker's continuing strengths as an eloquent elegiac poet, taking great risks within the romantic convention of the poet as divine scapegoat, were recognised again. And his *Collected Poems*, edited by Robert Fraser in 1987, for all their occasional lapses into heady and parodiable rhetoric, confirmed that here was a poet whose range was impressively wide, not only rhetorical but often proverbially plain. A year after his death, *Street Songs* showed his power, as well as his glaring faults, as clearly and memorably as his debut sixty years earlier.

David Gascoyne, who emerged precociously with his first book of poems when he was only sixteen, who pioneered Surrealism in England in the 1930s, and whose *Poems 1937–1942* was one of the best books produced during the Second World War, has published very little indeed in the years covered by this survey; but it is worth noticing that in spite of this there has been a renewed interest in his work recently, particularly among young people – part of a reassessment of, and fashion for, Surrealism, to some extent nurtured in the universities and colleges of art.

To some, W.S. Graham (who first came to notice as part of the so-called 'New Apocalypse' in the 1940s) became an equally interesting figure, and one who continued to publish, and to change, until his death in 1986. Though his *Malcolm Mooney's Land* (1970) spoke in the same riddling, mesmerised voice he had long established, *Implements in Their Places* (1977), though oracular, was plainer; and his *Collected Poems 1942–1977* (1979) put him in perspective as a more interestingly developing writer than once seemed likely. Something of the same sort could be said about Lawrence Durrell, whose career as a poet can be seen as split between his pre-war and 1940s reputation as a fastidious classic-romantic, drawing on a Mediterranean historical/hedonistic terrain, and the later poems, after his international fame as a novelist of the Alexandria Quartet in the 1950s. (His travel books, such as *Prospero's Cell* and *Bitter Lemons*, are better associated with the poems than with these novels.) His *Collected Poems 1931–1974* (1980) indeed show him at his peak in that earlier work; but there are a few later poems (such as 'A Patch of Dust', written in 1974) which beautifully catch the old freshness. When he died in 1990, several obituarists drew attention to his fine poems, at the expense of the Quartet and later novels, seeing Durrell as a brilliant celebrator of the fusion of past and present, rather than the showy and sometimes spurious entertainer who transmogrified Alexandria into an often ponderous raree show.

Durrell had a taste for what Anthony Burgess called 'the corruption of the exotic'. Norman Nicholson had no such inclination. His poems, from their beginnings in the 1940s, were almost totally absorbed in the landscapes, characters and ancestries of his native Cumberland, where he always lived, being born and – almost – dying in the same house. These poems had an authenticity and substance which was recognised and praised in his last two books. *A Local Habitation* (1972) and *Sea to the West* (1981), sharing some of his fellow-Cumbrian Wordsworth's concerns without being dominated by them – as in 'On the Dismantling of Millom Ironworks':

And maybe the ghost of Wordsworth, seeing further than I can,
Will stare from Duddon Bridge, along miles of sand and mud-
   flats
To a peninsula bare as it used to be, and, beyond, to a river
Flowing, untainted now, to a bleak, depopulated shore.

Nicholson, who died in 1987, has a fine posthumous monument in the form of a *Collected Poems* (1994), well edited by Neil Curry.

6

Stevie Smith, Geoffrey Grigson, Roy Fuller, Gavin Ewart, Charles Causley

Stevie Smith was a complete original. Someone writing soon after her death in 1971 commented that she was like William Blake rewritten by Ogden Nash, but though that is quite smart it doesn't really catch her unique mixture of whimsical gloom, eccentric common sense, incantation, nursery rhyme, doggerel and rhythmical subtlety. Towards the end of her life (and she spent sixty-five years of it living in the same house in an unfashionable part of north London), she wrote that she felt 'as if I were looking through a beautiful window at a distance that is full of amiability but has cast a spell. I do not mind this, in fact rather like it.' That is very much the note of Stevie Smith's poetry – a note not often heard in modern poetry. Indeed, when she first tried to publish her poems in the mid-1930s she found little enthusiasm for them. It was only gradually that she came to be recognised as a very special poet of strangeness, loneliness and quirky humour, particularly with her *Selected Poems* of 1962 and the Penguin selection published in the same year (1966) as *The Frog Prince*.

Stevie Smith often made poems out of fancies and odd imaginings which might have seemed to anyone else unpromising and quite unpoetic, such as the lines:

Do take Muriel out
She is looking so glum
Do take Muriel out
All her friends have gone

[. . .]

Do take Muriel out
Although your name is Death

('Do Take Muriel Out')

Stevie Smith
BBC

She was always a poet concerned with death, and during her
last years it had been her central theme – not really gloomy,
but seen in an almost sprightly way: Death as something to be
comfortably welcomed, like a neighbour.

I have a friend
At the end
Of the world.
His name is a breath

Of fresh air.
He is dressed in
Grey chiffon. At least
I think it is chiffon.

It has a
Peculiar look, like smoke.

('Black March')

The quality of her poems was immensely enhanced by her own
reading (or often chanting or singing) of them: her readings
became her poems, with her inimitable blend of levity, loneliness,
and sometimes asperity. She could sustain a narrative (as in
'Angel Boley'), indulge in sly theological polemics ('How do
you see the Holy Spirit of God?'), be bewilderingly whimsical
('Mrs Blow and Her Animals') or quietly poignant ('Oblivion'),
and her humour was often offhand and mocking:

The foolish poet wonders
Why so much honour
Is given to other poets
But to him
No honour is given.

('The Poet Hin')

Her *Collected Poems* (edited by James MacGibbon) appeared
in 1975, and since then there has been a good deal of both
biographical and critical work. Her 'seriousness' and
'importance' are still questioned by some (was she naive, or
faux-naif? Childish or childlike? Ingenuous or disingenuous?);
but the consensus is that she was indeed an important original,
an idiosyncratic and often very funny entertainer who drew on
many invented voices.

The sort of pretensions Stevie Smith sometimes mocked
were even more extensively and scathingly treated in some of
Geoffrey Grigson's poems. When he was editor of *New Verse*
in the 1930s, his activities with what he has called the 'billhook'
cut down the pompous, the fatuous, the obscurantist, the
careerist and the dim in large and bloody swathes. He could

be memorably contemptuous – of a *cause célèbre* involving a
well-known Scottish poet, for example:

Because MacOssian thieves what other men have written
Detested bullying Englishmen abuse him.
Why not, when only reiving
Lallans-leaking Scots excuse him?

('Master of Aleatory Verse')★

Or of a literary lord who renounced his peerage:

Peers have been made whose hired robes have hidden
A depth of wallowing in the dirtiest midden.
Here was a lord – his hopes and head were both too big –
Who doffed his ermine and revealed a pig.

('On a Change of Style')★

But though these epigrams, together with snarls and brief
fits of petulance against 'smart reviewers', 'Journalist-dons,
hair-oiled ad-men', and the inanities of television culture, were
characteristic of one side of Grigson's personality in his poetry,
they were not dominant. Most of the poems in his two collected
volumes (published 1963 and 1982) are sensuous notations of
places, people and very closely observed scenes, celebrations
of the oddity and variety of natural life. It is the passionate
naturalist, archaeologist, topographer and traveller that watched
from the centre of many of Grigson's poems, restlessly
particularising and recording:

An item of best being is
Halving this pear and in its

Ivory seeing this black
Star of seeds.

Also pointing this black
Star in ivory out to you,
And you agreeing, is
An item of best being.

('Halving of a Pear')

Such plainness can be almost pedestrian. Conversely, in
other poems Grigson could be sometimes finically intense, so
concerned with precise shades of colour, textures, quiddities, that
the effect is static and cluttered. But his talent for enjoyment,
even when it turned bitter or waspish, was one that genuinely
communicates a sense of the unrepeatable moment. Right up
to the end (he died in 1985 at the age of eighty), Grigson wrote
quirkily – of pleasures, memories, wonders and, as always,
sharply of things and people he despised and loathed. His
posthumously published book *Persephone's Flowers* contains 'The
Dipper'*:

Staring down from that broken, one-arched bridge,
In that vale of water-mint, saint, lead-mine and midge,
I was amazed by that fat black-and-white water bird
Hunting under the current, not at all disturbed.

How could I tell that what I saw then and there
Would live for me still in my eightieth year?

Roy Fuller's poems began to appear during the 1930s, in such
magazines as Grigson's *New Verse*. They had a pretty strong
taste of Auden about them, and were witty, intelligent, rather
dry, very much aware of what was going on in the political
world around him but having a wry detachment as well.

Though he went on to write better poems than these, such qualities continued to hold good in Fuller's work. It was with his first volume of *Collected Poems* (1962) that it was generally recognised that Fuller had authoritatively become one of the leading poets in the generation immediately following that of Auden – quite different from the 'alternative romanticism' of Dylan Thomas and George Barker, but having a forceful integrity of its own, capable of eloquent phrase-making as well as dryly witty cerebration, as in the monologue 'The Ides of March', the sequences 'Mythological Sonnets', 'To X' and 'Meredithian Sonnets', or, in miniature, one of the 'Bagatelles'*:

A pale leaf floats and falls, and instantly
Is pasted on the concrete by a tyre.
The world betrays its wobble from the fire;
The giant orbit deigned to cut the tree.

Fuller developed a capacity for rich and resonant thinking-aloud in verse, and a technical ability which showed itself in a whole range of forms working out a shaping and phrase-making imagination. But it was after the first *Collected Poems*, in his *New Poems* (1968), that he showed an even more striking development, in which his strict forms and ingenious rhymes were largely jettisoned and the voice became deceptively relaxed and low-keyed, allowing moments of blankness and self-disgust or facetiousness to be caught entirely without straining pose or frigid distancing:

Girl with fat legs, reading Georgette Heyer,
Shall I arrange you in my pantheon?

('Romance')

Is it possible that anyone so silly can
Write anything good?

('Last Sheet')

If I became penniless tomorrow . . .
Still impossible to change to a hero of art!

('Chinoiserie')

These quotations from three different poems show a nakedness
of address risky in its fidelity. But these low and absurd
self-observations modulate quite naturally and with suppleness
into something graver, more elevated and more eloquent:
Fuller earns the right to this through plotting his progression.
Thus the first quotation – a snobbish mock-rhetorical flourish
– begins both by disarming one and making one prickle with
embarrassment, but ends:

Return, great goddesses, and your society
Where even little girls develop
Strong superegos, and the misfortune
Of woman's weak moral nature is unknown;
And the wars are waged on a lower epicycle
By armour diminutive as stag beetles;
And poets forbidden to sing of their diseases
Or amatory botherations;
And only with end-stopped irony.

('Romance')

Without being academic (he was actually a very successful
company lawyer, and a rare example of the poet as
businessman), Fuller was an alert, very widely read, endlessly
curious and unashamedly intellectual poet. More than any poet
since Auden, he used his reading of Freud and Jung in trying to
make sense of human drives and infirmities, and he had a strong
sense of history. As a young man, and well into maturity,
he had been much taken with Marxist theories about history
and about economics, though he later discarded them. In his

sequence of sonnets 'The Historian', Fuller's persona considers 'the notion of the Wall and Counter Wall' in ancient Syracuse, and concludes:

> I see at every crucial turn of fate
> Those soldier labourers, those citizen-
> Victims at their crass, suicidal tricks;
> And find, to say the least, inadequate
> The rueful groans that rose on all sides when
> They turned from love or art to handle bricks.

Fuller's enduring monument is likely to be his *New and Collected Poems 1934–84* (1985), though this was followed by three further volumes before his death in 1991, and then a posthumous volume edited by his son. These *Last Poems* (1993) show that almost to the end Fuller was writing as clearly, and sometimes as poignantly, as ever:

> Most of the inconveniences of my
> Demise will not, however, be borne by me –
> Consoling, now that almost anything
> Unusual brings with it anxiety.
>
> Often I feel perhaps I don't mind death –
> Still free from pain and lameness, despite old age;
> And yet I blench to think some moment in
> The story I shan't be there to turn the page.

> ('The Story')★

Gavin Ewart's poems fall into two long-separated periods. He had a precocious start: some of his work appeared in *New Verse* when he was still a schoolboy in the early 1930s, and his first book (*Poems and Songs*, 1938) had a cheeky freshness, full of the lighter side of Auden – the four lines about Miss Twye soaping her breasts in the bath have become favourite anthology material. Then there was silence, only sporadically interrupted, for over twenty years, until a succession of Ewart publications began to appear in the mid-1960s. The odd thing is that the revivified Ewart turns out to be recognisably the same as the old, his humour blacker and more scabrous than before, perhaps, but then the 1960s were famously 'permissive' times. The formal structures of the poems – their shapes and sizes – are dashingly various: Ewart himself has said that 'the more technical expertise goes into a poem, as a general rule, the more interesting it is'.

Ewart's prolific succession of books since 1966 has been gathered into *The Collected Ewart 1933–1980* (1980) and a second large volume, *Collected Poems 1980–1990* (1991); but even these do not account for everything, such as the selections of very short poems he has produced in recent years. In Ewart, high spirits, low humour, black farce and affectionate melancholy all combine: sometimes one of these is in the ascendant, sometimes another. He is not primarily interested in 'importance' (certainly not if it has to be of a solemn kind), and it may well be that, as he himself has written,

> by writing the one-line sagas
> and fooling about with the norm
> the Poet Ewart may have answered
> the vexing Question of Form.

His inventiveness and virtuosity frequently grapple with the delights and absurdities of sex, but also with literary politics, misprints, the oddities of ordinary modern urban life, random wartime memories of his life as a conscript officer, the anthropology of offices, and a great deal else. It is partly a matter of scale:

> The death of a mouse from cancer is the whole sack
> of Rome by the Goths,
> the end of the British Empire is the munching of
> coats by some moths,

the smallness of any action doesn't stop it from being
the same
as anything big or bigger – it's just the scale, and the
name.

('The Death of a Mouse')*

Finding material everywhere and anywhere, Ewart rummages
among the newspaper small ads, discovers 'found poems'
on public notices and in public lavatories, revels in abstruse
glossaries, writes in rhyming Latin or invented American
demotic. And the humour, the unpretentiousness, the
unexpectedness, add up to an imaginative abundance which can't
be pushed into the margin, or patronised. Philip Larkin wrote
of his 'well-shaped pieces, freaked with pain and absurdity', and
of this 'astonishing, unstoppable talent . . . And this is what
underlies his claim on our attention, this ability to pull out of
the bag a new Ewart'.

Although Charles Causley's first collection of poems was
not published until 1951, he began writing during the war
when he was in the navy, and over forty years later the sea
is still often present in his work. The sea-shanty, the ballad,
the jaunty narrative have always been his forms, outwardly
simple, often humorous, always bright and melodious. But
his range has widened and deepened, as can be seen from
his two substantial volumes of *Collected Poems* (1975, then
1992).

Causley's earlier brisk ballads sometimes seem a little too
resolutely jolly, but he isn't the simple old-fashioned lyrical
soul some people take him for. In 'Ballad of the Bread Man',
for instance, the lively step of the verse is quite clearly and
deliberately working against what it is actually saying, and the
contrast is a large part of the effect:

Mary stood in the kitchen
Baking a loaf of bread.
An angel flew in through the window.
'We've a job for you', he said.

Even when the verse is reduced to something very like doggerel, as in 'I Saw a Jolly Hunter', the effect is a sophisticated one, calling on memories of nursery rhymes to give the poem irony. Causley has a grander, more measured manner too, often drawing on the personal and circumstantial, with the old lyrical sweetness but with new depths – at the end of 'Conducting a Children's Choir':

> I bait the snapping breath, curled claw, the deep
> And delicate tongue that lends no man its aid.
> The children their unsmiling kingdoms keep,
> And I walk with them, and I am afraid.

His hospital poems (for example 'Ten Types of Hospital Visitor') and about his mother's final illness and death have a rapt observation and a sane steadiness:

> One, bird-like, lifting up her blinded head
> To sounds beyond the television-blare
> Cries out, in a sharp sliver of a voice,
> *I do not know if anyone is there!*
>
> I do not know if anyone is here.
> If so, if not so, I must let it be.
> I hold your drifted hand; no time to tell
> What six dead women hear, or whom they see.

> ('Six Women')

There is, indeed, a great deal more art in Causley's work than may appear at first sight. There is also a wider compass of experience, drawing in more recent years on travels in Australia, Israel and elsewhere; but in essence Causley has no need to travel to find experience – it is close to him, in his sense of place in his native Cornwall, in his rootedness in the humane discipline of thirty years teaching in local schools. Commonsense and celebration coexist in his sane and memorable poems.

7

The 'Movement' and after

The 'Movement' – as can be gathered at magisterial length from Blake Morrison's 1980 book of that title – is, or was, a complex phenomenon. Was it a true literary happening of the 1950s, or an invention by journalists? If it existed, who belonged to it? And did it achieve anything, or was it (as Ian Hamilton has put it) something with 'its distinctive niche in the history of publicity – it was a take-over bid and it brilliantly succeeded'?

This survey, which takes as its starting point the early 1960s, is not the place to plot the first moves in the campaign (if one accepts Hamilton's notion that there was a campaign), nor its supposed documents of the 1950s – the anthologies *Poets of the 1950s* and *New Lines*, the poetry magazine *Listen*, the review columns of the *Spectator*, and so on. When Robert Conquest edited *New Lines 2* in 1963, he remarked in his Introduction that Donald Davie had suggested that a suitable title for the section containing poems by the original figures (Kingsley Amis, D.J. Enright, Thom Gunn, Elizabeth Jennings, Philip Larkin, John Wain, and Conquest and Davie themselves) might be 'Divergent Lines'; and one takes the point. And if *New Lines 2* could include Ted Hughes (as it did), wasn't it in fact embracing the 'dynamic romanticism' that critics of the Old Movement had called for?

But Ian Hamilton raised a question concerning one member of this supposed Movement, in his article 'The Making of the Movement' (collected in *A Poetry Chronicle*, 1973):

> At one level, it could be said that Philip Larkin's poems provide a precise model for what the Movement was supposed to be seeking. But having noted his lucidity, his debunkery, his technical accomplishment and other such 'typical' attributes, one would still be left with the different and deeper task of describing the quality of his peculiar genius . . .

Philip Larkin
Philip Sayer

In his lifetime, Larkin's achievement was recognised even by
critics who were suspicious of his supposed 'attitudes' and who
were contemptuous of most or all of the other poets who were
enlisted with him into the Movement. This was made clear in
the years following the publication of *The Less Deceived* (1955),
his first mature book, and of *New Lines*, and it was confirmed
by the publication at ten-year intervals of his two later books
of poems. As Andrew Motion has put it: '*The Less Deceived*
made his name; *The Whitsun Weddings* made him famous; *High
Windows* turned him into a national monument'.

But it was not until his death at the end of 1985 that the
strength of devotion of Larkin's readership was made plain – for
example, in the enormous congregation which came together for
his memorial service in Westminster Abbey in February 1986.
The publication of his *Collected Poems* in 1988, adding over
eighty poems to the Larkin canon, showed chronologically

the curve from prolific adolescence in the 1930s (when he was largely dominated by Auden), through the yearning Yeatsianism that held him until the late 1940s, and then most strikingly the acquisition of his own voice, or voices, until the drought of his later years. The book was an immediate success, going into many impressions; though there were some who thought that Larkin's own careful ordering of poems within individual volumes had been irretrievably tampered with.

Innocence, the pathos and grim humour of experience, the poignancy of the past (whether one's own remembered past or the imagined past of another century), the change and renewal of nature, the dread of the future, death and all that leads up to it and away from it: such listing of the subject-matter of Larkin's poems quickly runs itself into flat abstractions, totally lacking the precise circumstantial figurativeness and sensitive cadences of the poems themselves. Larkin said that a good poem is both 'sensitive' and 'efficient' – two more abstractions, but ones that are given flesh when one reads such poems as 'The Building', 'The Old Fools', 'Sad Steps', 'The Explosion', 'The Whitsun Weddings', 'An Arundel Tomb'. 'The Building' opens with a typically dense and carefully selected proliferation of impressionist detail, so organised that it is only gradually one realises that the place being described is a hospital: as in 'Church Going' and 'The Whitsun Weddings', the detail is an embodiment of the poem, not the casual decoration its colloquial ease at first suggests:

                    on the way
    Someone's wheeled past, in washed-to-rags ward clothes:
    They see him, too. They're quiet. To realise
    This new thing held in common makes them quiet,
    For past these doors are rooms, and rooms past those,
    And more rooms yet, each one further off

    And harder to return from

And in the end, relentlessly poised like the train in 'The Whitsun Weddings', the realisation towards which the whole delicate structure has been aimed is achieved:

All know they are going to die.
Not yet, perhaps not here, but in the end,
And somewhere like this. That is what it means,
This clean-sliced cliff; a struggle to transcend
The thought of dying, for unless its powers
Outbuild cathedrals nothing contravenes
The coming dark, though crowds each evening try

With wasteful, weak, propitiatory flowers.

The stanzaic and rhymed structure of 'The Building', typically,
is so unobtrusive, draws so little superficial attention to itself,
that only a closer look reveals how tightly organised it is. Each
seven-line stanza is completely consistent in its rhyme scheme,
but the first line of each stanza picks up the rhyme in the fifth
line of the stanza preceding it, so that the whole poem can be
seen to be made up of interlinked quatrains (ABCB: DCAD),
the 'trailing' rhyme picking up the serpentine movement and
running it on. To those who may think such considerations
trivial, mere fingering of an old-fashioned instrument, there are
many possible answers: one is that it works.

   Sometimes Larkin dealt with his habitual themes of
diminution, decay, death, in an extreme and even savage way,
as he did in 'Sunny Prestatyn', in which the blandishments of
the girl on the poster have been desecrated and disproved. The
opening of 'The Old Fools' – looking at geriatric patients in
what is, in ordinary euphemistic terms, called 'an old people's
home' – has something of the same feeling:

What do they think has happened, the old fools,
To make them like this? Do they somehow suppose
It's more grown-up when your mouth hangs open and drools,
And you keep on pissing yourself, and can't remember
Who called this morning?

But such savagery always turns back on itself in Larkin, and is often seen with fear and horror. The triumph is that of art. Clive James has written of him that he is 'the poet of the void. The one affirmation his work offers is the possibility that when we have lost everything the problem of beauty will still remain.'

Even Larkin's least elevated, most casually light poems have a refined, unobtrusive, but technically formidable skill, able to accommodate colloquial language and colloquial rhythms: 'Posterity', for example, which casts a cold eye on 'Jake Balokowsky, my biographer', and 'Vers de Société', which balances boring sociability against the pleasures and desolation of solitude. Both serious and light have the distinctive, sad, subtle and palpable flavour of an individual with the loyalties, exasperations, prejudices, illuminations and speaking voice of a distinctly irreducible character.

Part of Larkin's breadth of appeal comes from the many kinds of poem this character can appear in. There is the impersonal but raptly detailed evocation of nineteenth-century emigrants ('How Distant') or of earlier-twentieth-century colliers ('The Explosion'); there is the narrative meditation, the extended anecdote, in which the poet is at the centre of a particular experience, precisely delineated, but at the same time contriving to speak for all ('Church Going', 'The Whitsun Weddings'); there are those poems in which the poet is openly, outrageously there, delivering shocking, grim and grimly funny proverbial wisdoms, new-minted dreadful truths ('High Windows', 'Annus Mirabilis', 'Sad Steps', 'Self's the Man', 'This be the Verse'). Only very occasionally – most savagely and desperately in 'Love Again', which Larkin did not publish in his lifetime – does he speak personally from the centre of an emotional situation. And there is the detached lyrical naturalism of 'Cut Grass' and 'The Trees':

The trees are coming into leaf
Like something almost being said;
The recent buds relax and spread,
Their greenness is a kind of grief.

Is it that they are born again

And we grow old? No, they die too.
Their yearly trick of looking new
Is written down in rings of grain.

Yet still the unresting castles thresh
In fullgrown thickness every May.
Last year is dead, they seem to say,
Begin afresh, afresh, afresh.

('The Trees')★

Individual though Larkin was, he often reflected common
experiences and common concerns. In a broadcast introduction
to a selection of his poems in 1958, he wrote:

> Certainly the poems I write are bound up with the life I
> lead and the kind of person I am. But I don't think this
> makes them superficial; I think it improves them. If I
> avoid abstractions such as are found in politics and religion
> it's because they have never affected me strongly enough
> to become part of my personal life, and so cease being
> abstractions.

As far as 'public' concerns go, he touched on such things
in some poems (such as 'Going, Going' and 'Homage to a
Government'), showing attitudes that were conservative, even
'reactionary' – in this, though in little else, reminding one of
Yeats and Eliot. After his death, the publication of his *Selected
Letters* in 1992 and of Andrew Motion's *Philip Larkin: A
Writer's Life* in 1993 provoked in some quarters a combination
of outraged 'political correctness', sanctimonious priggishness,
and an attempt to relegate his work and his reputation to the
margins. Often those who condemned him failed to see that
Larkin's alleged misogyny, racism, and (as he put it) 'knee-jerk
reactions' were (as he also put it) 'gouts of bile' – an instinctive
rancorous impatience with himself and the world. In the letters,
and in his conversation, these were ways of entertaining and

provoking his readers and his listeners, often with mordant and lugubrious humour. Those who fail to understand this also tend to fail to understand his poems. It may be that, for a time, those who have led the campaign to belittle Larkin will have some success, at least in the more censorious uphills of Academe. But among ordinary people – the audience which he hoped to reach, and indeed reached, in his lifetime – Larkin's poems are still read with affection and insight, not only in Britain, but far beyond.

The coarse, genial, unillusioned talent of Kingsley Amis is very like one facet of Larkin's – that side of Larkin which delivered itself of such statements as 'Get stewed. Books are a load of crap.' Amis and Larkin were close friends from their Oxford undergraduate days in the 1940s; and Larkin's correspondence with Amis over forty-odd years is a remarkable literary monument in its own right. Amis manages the stylish jeer very well, in his poems as in his prose fiction. The worm's-eye-view commemorated in his sequence 'The Evans Country' entertainingly exposes hypocrisies and furtive sexual goings-on of all sorts, grinning, unjudging, triumphant. The hypocrisies are pretensions about art as well as about morality:

> Hearing how tourists, dazed with reverence,
> Looked through sunglasses at the Parthenon,
> Dai thought of that cold night outside the Gents
> When he touched Dilys up with his gloves on.

> ('Aldport [Mystery Tour]')★

In this narrow area of 'come off it', Amis's touch is as sure as Dai's. But his *Collected Poems 1944–1979*, gathering the best of his handful of slim volumes, showed a wider range than this: the laconic, moving assurance of the early 'Lessons' and 'Masters'; the romantic unromanticism of 'Wrong Words', 'A Dream of Fair Women' and, indeed, 'Against Romanticism'; the epigrammatic good humour, matched with narrative meditativeness, of 'A Bookshop Idyll' and 'A Song of Experience'; and the mockingly grim confrontations with death – 'Shitty', 'Lovely', 'Drinking Song'. His Gravesian pastiches are little more than that, and he has too easily been a self-caricaturist; but his best poems are lasting emblems to the best of the Movement.

The most unlikely poet to be corralled into the Movement was Elizabeth Jennings. She was the sole woman; she was not an academic but worked in a public library (even Larkin was a *university* librarian); she was a devout Christian, a Roman Catholic. What perhaps partly helped to enlist her, to make both Robert Conquest and D.J. Enright feel that she belonged with the others in their anthologies, was her sense of order, of carefully resolved form. The very first poem in her first pamphlet and her first book, and reprinted as the first poem in her subsequent volumes of *Collected Poems* (1967 and 1986), is an early witness of this:

> The radiance of that star that leans on me
> Was shining years ago. The light that now
> Glitters up there my eye may never see,
> And so the time lag teases me with how
>
> Love that loves now may not reach me until
> Its first desire is spent. The star's impulse
> Must wait for eyes to claim it beautiful
> And love arrived may find us somewhere else.

('Delay')★

Over all the years that have followed, she has worked almost doggedly at her contemplative, orderly gift, in poems which are rational but open to mystery, tender but usually unsentimental, expressed in forms and words that are almost always pure, clear, gravely lyrical, and committed to a sense of winning something seemly out of something chaotic. There have been times when one has sensed a thinning-away into a simplicity that can look like banality. But throughout her career, she has often produced poems of a naked directness which have something of the intensity of Emily Dickinson:

47

I feel I could be turned to ice
If this goes on, if this goes on.
I feel I could be buried twice
And still the death not yet be done.

I feel I could be turned to fire
If there can be no end to this.
I know within me such desire
No kiss could satisfy, no kiss.

I feel I could be turned to stone,
A solid block not carved at all.
Because I feel so much alone,
I could be grave-stone or a wall.

But better to be turned to earth
Where other things at least can grow.
I could be then a part of birth,
Passive, not knowing how to know.

('I Feel')★

D.J. Enright's poems are quite different: loose, discursive,
amusing, commonsensical, serious but amiable, throwaway
in their wanly indignant annotations of social brutalities
and masqueradings in a world that stretches, if not from
China to Peru, then from Thailand to the English Midlands.
Enright's poems seem to wander through the world, sometimes
bemused as well as amused, grumbling, punning, taking a
liberal-humanist view of things but usually tinged with irony:

A shabby old man is mixing water with clay.
If that shabby old man had given up hope
(He is probably tired: he has worked all day)
The flimsy house would never have been built.

If the flimsy house had never been built
Six people would shiver in the autumn breath.
If thousands of shabby old men were sorry as you
Millions of people would cough themselves to death.

(In the town the pin-ball parlours sing like cicadas)
Do not take refuge in some far-off foreign allusion
(In the country the cicadas ring like pin-ball parlours)
Simply remark the clay, the water, the straw, and a useful person.

('Broken Fingernails')★

He has also become a clever constructer of sequences; *The Terrible Shears* looked at his own upbringing as the son of an Irish immigrant, while *Paradise Illustrated* and *A Faust Book* were witty, downbeat variations on themes by Milton and Goethe:

'Why didn't we think of clothes before?'
Asked Adam,
Removing Eve's.

'Why did we ever think of clothes?'
Asked Eve,
Laundering Adam's.

(xxii from *Paradise Illustrated*)★

Of all the former members of the Movement, Donald Davie is the one who has tried most strenuously to detach himself from its supposed limitations. In a 1959 essay, 'Remembering the Movement', he accused himself and the others of being 'deprecating, ingratiating', openly confessing to opportunist motives. Davie's earlier poems are polished examples of

neo-Augustanism. Thereafter, he has gone through an almost
bewildering series of phases, embracing Ezra Pound, sounding
like a clever translation of Pasternak, garrulously using the
counties of England to make a curious tapestry of his country
and his own life. There has been a restlessness, even at times an
irritability, about all this; and indeed Davie is a difficult poet
from whom to quote accurately and justly. As early as 1959
– the year in which he decisively subtracted himself from the
Movement – his free adaptation of Mickiewicz's *Pan Tadeusz*
(*The Forests of Lithuania*) showed that he was not content to
remain what he himself called 'a pasticheur of late Augustan
styles'. He can be a sensuous, accurately visual relisher of the
world:

> Like a snake it is, its serpentine iridescence
> Of slow light spilt and wheeling over calm
> Inundations, and a snake's still menace
> Hooding with bruised sky belfry and lonely farm.

> ('Low Lands')

He can be didactically plain:

> The metaphysicality
> Of poetry, how I need it!
> And yet it was for years
> What I refused to credit.

> ('Or, Solitude')

He can be diffusely polemical:

> The bluff stuff. Double bluff when
> back from the Dardanelles

with lead in your lung, Ted Hughes
runs you for a long
still running season, rats
behind the industrial arras
of Mexborough, the pasteboard
Barnsley of grime and phlegm
hawked up, thrillingly mined with
rats and stoical killers.
The bluff stuff. Double bluff.
Brutal manners, brutal
simplifications as
we drag it all down.

('England 3')

Davie has an unsettled, sharply intelligent talent; but it somehow
lacks a centre. His large-scale volume of *Collected Poems* (1990)
takes one along a switchback of styles and attitudes.

Thom Gunn's *Collected Poems* (1993) shows him moving
from the tough, strict (he has called it 'clenched') style of his
early-1950s poems ('The Wound', 'Carnal Knowledge'), through
looser syllabic measures he acquired soon after he began his
long residence in the United States, and then into a variety of
styles which coexist. To some he will always be the almost
aggressively existentialist motorbike poet of 'On the Move':

At worst, one is in motion; and at best,
Reaching no absolute, in which to rest,
One is always nearer by not keeping still.

Indeed, he has always been a poet who makes active use of *pose*,
in matter as in manner – for example, the notorious lines:

I think of all the toughs through history
And thank heaven they lived, continually.

('Lines for a Book')

But the poses have adopted different postures – fixed, fluid, tense, relaxed. The broad span of techniques has been confident, from the beginning; and yet there has also been a continuing sense of vulnerability, and – increasingly – a sense of extraordinary purity, even innocence.

Such words may seem odd and inappropriate ones to use of someone who deals as Gunn has frequently, in his later poems, done with naked predatory homosexual passions. The new-found plague of AIDS has produced in him not only a plangent elegiac sense, but a sense of unjudging improvisation, of trying to see things as they are, to see happiness as coming from a childlike physical unity – temporary, vulnerable, threatened:

> The love of old men is not worth a lot,
> Desperate and dry even when it is hot.
> You cannot tell what is enthusiasm
> And what involuntary clawing spasm.

> ('Lines for my 55th Birthday')★

And the steady tread of his assured iambics, more than thirty years later, carry the full, earned weight of experience, as in the closing stanzas of 'The Missing', a poem written in 1987:

> But death – Their deaths have left me less defined:
> It was their pulsing presence made me clear.
> I borrowed from it, I was unconfined,
> Who tonight balance unsupported here,

> Eyes glaring from raw marble, in a pose
> Languorously part-buried in the block,
> Shins perfect and no calves, as if I froze
> Between potential and a finished work.

– Abandoned incomplete, shape of a shape,
In which exact detail shows the more strange,
Trapped in unwholeness, I find no escape
Back to the play of constant give and change.

The achievement of Gunn, seen as a whole in his magnificent
collected volume, is more impressive than any other of the
Movement poets, with the exception of Larkin. Gunn's progress,
over the years, has at times seemed less certain, more apt to
stand still or even take backward steps; but in perspective that
uncertainty looks like part of his strength.

8

Ted Hughes and Sylvia Plath

Since his first book, *The Hawk in the Rain* (1957), Ted Hughes
has been a prolific, much noticed, fascinating and often
bewildering poet. His marriage to, influence on, break with,
and (after her suicide in early 1963) continuing and troubled
executory relationship with Sylvia Plath have played a significant
part. So has his appointment as Poet Laureate in 1984, when
Philip Larkin turned down the invitation. Somehow Hughes
– a very private man, a complex bundle of commonsensical
Yorkshire and raptly mystical eclecticism – has weathered it all,
and survives as a potent, often enigmatic force in contemporary
British poetry.

But it has to be acknowledged that much of that force
comes from two particular clusters of his earlier work: the
'animal' poems, from his first book, from *Lupercal* (1960), and
to a smaller extent from *Wodwo* (1967); and the book-length
sequence *Crow* (1970). These established his place as a powerful
model for his contemporaries and juniors, someone whose
work concentrated on physical vividness of a mimetic sort,
in a turbulent world of predatory animals, primitive violence,
moments of extreme human endurance, mingled with narrative
elements of folk-tale, much reading of shamanistic and
pre-literate oral poetry. No matter what his later efforts have
been, including some very odd manifestations of his role as
Laureate, it is with these earlier works that he has made his
mark.

English poetry, from Chaucer to Larkin and beyond,
has tended to give primacy to the human, the ordinary, the
rational. Of course there have been large exceptions, most
prominently Spenser and Milton; but Shakespeare, Dryden,
Pope, Wordsworth, Tennyson, Browning, are figures one can
properly cite as examples of this – to which one adds Skelton,
Wyatt, Rochester, Crabbe, Cowper, Hardy, and dozens of other
poets who might seem unlikely allies. But here and there other
names present themselves: Blake, Hopkins, D.H. Lawrence. And

Ted Hughes
Niall McDairmid

it is here that Ted Hughes attaches himself to the argument.

He has allowed himself to be so attached. Even in his slighter productions, such as his *Flowers and Insects* (his 1986 slim volume, embellished with pictures by his long-time collaborator Leonard Baskin), the publisher stated in the blurb, presumably approved by Hughes, that the poems were 'no more mere "nature poetry" than the work of his predecessors in the English tradition, such as Blake and Lawrence'. Hughes has staked out for himself a tradition which is not concerned with humanity, civility, the rational or the analytical: instead, it is full of primordial struggle, primitivism, instinctiveness, the repetitions of worship and of folk-tales:

Water wanted to live
It went to the sun it came weeping back

Water wanted to live
It went to the trees they burned it came weeping back

('How Water Began to Play')

Crow, which was described when it was first published as
'the passages of verse from about the first two-thirds of what
was to have been an epic folk-tale', was an immediate cause
of controversy. To some it was a major poem, a work of
genius; the central symbol was 'a new hero' – though that may
have been ironically meant. Elsewhere there were some small
protesting noises about Hughes's 'apparently deliberate resort
to primitive hamfisted adjectives and trudging monosyllabic
phrases', and his 'mechanical, drugging repetition'. Whatever
the consensus, *Crow* has certainly entered the poetry-reading
consciousness, and its manner or manners have been widely
imitated, and even parodied – a firm indication that a work has
'arrived'.

   Crow basically has two characters – Crow himself and
God. Crow is resilient, resourceful, evasive, built to survive
every kind of disaster; he is a protean figure, but these are
his irreducible characteristics. God is sometimes his partner,
sometimes his adversary or rival, often a passive presence who
goes on sleeping while Crow gets up to his gruesome tricks:

Crow laughed.
He bit the Worm, God's only son,
Into two writhing halves.

He stuffed into man the tail half
With the wounded end hanging out.

He stuffed the head half headfirst into woman
And it crept in deeper and up
To peer out through her eyes
Calling its tail-half to join up quickly, quickly
Because O it was painful.

('A Childish Prank')

The manner of *Crow* is almost all like this – a series of unmodified narrative accounts of brutally comic (or just brutally brutal) events, sometimes varied with catalogues of incantations or lists of questions ('Who . . .?', 'Where . . .?'), all of which are common devices in oral poetry from the pre-literate world – a genre one knows Hughes admires, and indeed 'Two Eskimo Songs' form part of the *Crow* sequence.

This kind of procedure – which some critics, trying to find some phenomenon nearer twentieth-century Britain to which to relate *Crow*, have likened to the technique of the horror-comic, with its crude devices of 'BAM! SPLAT! ZOWY!' – is a compendious one. Anything, so long as it lacks verbal or rhythmical subtlety and is painted in primary colours, can fit into it. But what is *Crow* about, beyond its manner? Some have answered 'Survival' – that of the merest subsistence, against mercilessly inimical forces. More nearly, it seems to me, it poses in aggressive terms an old-fashioned theology or demonology – a Manichean duality which Augustine would have recognised; did, in fact, recognise, and rejected because it was simple-minded in its refusal to see the world in other than dogmatically pessimistic and exclusive terms – arbitrary, unarguable, assuming an esoteric revelation that by-passes reason and substitutes assertion for truth:

Crow realised there were two Gods –

One of them much bigger than the other
Loving his enemies
And having all the weapons.

('Crow's Theology')

The ambiguities in this are all in the interpretation, never in the assertion: in this, Hughes in a sense puts himself beyond criticism. But judged solely as technical constructs, the *Crow* poems can properly be called monotonous, relying as they do on endless repetitions of a few rhetorical devices and a few key words (black, blood, smashed, stabbed, screamed). As with the paintings of Francis Bacon, a totality of horror is narrowly and intensely insisted, and in the end pays low dividends, because the trick, once noticed, is a diminishing one. Language is no longer a medium but a message, and the world is no longer something to be particularised (as it was in *The Hawk in the Rain* and *Lupercal*) but is retreated from. It is an abnegation not only from poetry but from wisdom.

Since *Crow*, Hughes has been more prolific than ever. *Cave Birds* (sub-titled resonantly but unilluminatingly as 'An Alchemical Cave Drama') is a sequence of twenty-nine poems written to accompany drawings by Leonard Baskin (whose menacing pictures of crows originally inspired *Crow*) of anthropomorphic imaginary birds, and can be seen as an extension of *Crow's* emblematic symbolism. *Season Songs* was bracketed off by Hughes's publishers as 'for children', but this modestly diminishing description does not disguise the poems' concentration, vividness and attack, or their more relaxed extension of the keen-eyed poet of *Lupercal* sixteen years earlier: 'The Stag', a cumulatively dramatic and moving picture of a stag hunt, and 'Swifts' are among his very best poems. *Gaudete* is held by a few devoted Hughes disciples to be the peak of his achievement; but to many others this long treatment of an Anglican clergyman possessed by 'powers of the other world' is a ludicrous travesty, unrelieved by the 'Epilogue' of verses at the end supposedly written by the Reverend Lumb. *Remains of Elmet* was another work that took its support from a visual source, this time photographs by Fay Godwin of parts of the Pennine moorland of Yorkshire where Hughes spent much of his childhood. Some of its component poems come to grips splendidly with the bleak topography and history of this landscape, a mixture of natural beauty and derelict industrialism:

> Streets bent to the task
> Of holding it all up
> Bracing themselves, taking the strain
> Till their vertebrae slipped.

> ('When Men got to the Summit')

Moortown is a sort of hold-all, with four books (or sequences) in one set of covers. The first, 'Moortown' itself, includes some of Hughes's finest poems, its material relating to that of *Season Songs*. In a note in the volume, it was typically played down by Hughes as being 'made up of passages taken from a verse farming diary that I kept for a while'. The setting is rural Devon, where Hughes has lived for many years. The word 'diary' is perhaps meant to allow for informality, even casualness, but many of the poems themselves have a degree of intensity, sanity and rapt grace that he has never equalled, as in 'February 17th', a powerfully resolute and exact account of delivering a lamb which had to be killed to save the mother:

> Then like
> Pulling myself to the ceiling with one finger
> Hooked in a loop, timing my effort
> To her birth push groans, I pulled against
> The corpse that would not come. Till it came.
> And after it the long, sudden, yolk-yellow
> Parcel of life
> In a smoking slither of oils and soups and syrups –
> And the body lay born, beside the hacked off head.

> ('February 17th')

The other three sections in *Moortown* are 'Prometheus on his Crag', 'Adam and the Sacred Nine', and 'Earth-numb'. All are further cryptic texts drawing on myths and using the same bare rhetorical devices as the *Crow* poems, with the same portentous grimness but without even their occasional flashes of primitive humour. Hughes has a copious and impressive talent – there is no doubt about that; but it is a talent which seems to change direction, soar, lose height, lose itself, recover, and then inexplicably repeat its own worst faults, again and again.

Wolfwatching (1989) marks a return, though in Hughes's later fragmented style, to his attentive observation of creatures, as did *Flowers and Insects*, which may be chiefly remarkable for one of its longest poems, 'Eclipse', which begins:

> For half an hour, through a magnifying glass,
> I've watched the spiders making love undisturbed,
> Ignorant of the voyeur, horribly happy.

This is a sustained piece of meticulous description of 'the famous murder'. *Rain-Charm for the Duchy and other Laureate Poems* (1992) brings on a wealth of weathers and creatures spun together with much mystical, mythical, historical underpinning of Hughes's 'complete vision of royalty and nationhood', as the blurb puts it. This is surprising stuff, at a time when royal marriages and affairs are under constant prurient scrutiny, and when the monarchy itself seems vulnerable. But, as usual, Hughes is not concerned with fashion: he can be (and is) mocked for his mannerisms, and nowadays is more parodied than imitated. And yet he cannot be ignored.

Hughes's work is inextricably linked with that of his first wife, Sylvia Plath. In a way, Hughes's poems are the *animus* to her *anima* – the male principle backing on to the female principle on the same coin: compare, for example, his 'Thistles' with her 'Mushrooms'. Sylvia Plath died towards the beginning of the period with which this essay deals, but her work appeared in posthumous books throughout the next decade and has gained a considerable following, even a cult of impassioned believers and commentators. She is still very much a live force in English poetry, into which has been woven an extremist legend of a doomed artist bent on self-destruction. The hysteria, memorialising aggrandizement, interpretative ludicrousness and plain bad judgement of what has been called 'the Plath industry' are unpleasantly reminiscent of the ballyhoo that followed the death of Dylan Thomas ten years earlier. It seems not so much that art needs its victims but that the susceptible reading public does.

Sylvia Plath's posthumously published *Ariel* (1965) is the crucial collection, now fully augmented and placed in its context in the *Collected Poems* (1981). The poems that have had most attention have naturally enough been those in *Ariel*, because there has been more time to assimilate them; but because much of that book was written during the downward spin which brought her to her suicide, it is unbalanced to think of her as most importantly the poet of such death-infatuated pieces as 'Daddy' and 'Lady Lazarus' – these were the final spurts of lava from the volcano. The volcano image may seem as hysterical as the responses I have just been chiding, but it is meant to convey the feeling in Plath's work of dormant pressure: most of her poems are the wisps of smoke above the cone, indicating but not embodying the violence below. A large number of them are vividly and warmly celebratory, intent on what Barbara Hardy has called 'imaginative enlargement' – of candles, for example:

I watch their spilt tears cloud and dull to pearls.
How shall I tell anything at all
To this infant still in a birth-drowse?
Tonight, like a shawl, the mild light enfolds her,
The shadows stoop over like guests at a christening.

('Candles')

Or of an old man convalescing (in 'Among the Narcissi'):

There is a dignity to this; there is a formality —
The flowers vivid as bandages, and the man mending.
They bow and stand: they suffer such attacks!

And the octogenarian loves the little flocks.
He is quite blue; the terrible wind tries his breathing.
The narcissi look up like children, quickly and whitely.

In these poems, and in many others in *Crossing the Water and Winter Trees* as well as *Ariel*, she is very far from being that patron saint of the nervous breakdown which her imitators would have her be. The felt life, the exuberant observation, the freshness and efficiency of her sensuous apprehension of the world flash out and blossom again and again. This is not to diminish the serious intensity of her obsessively disturbed poems but to put them in their proper perspective as statements that are no more 'final' (except in a chronological sense) than the rest of her prolific output. She was a remarkably poised and controlled poet, and we do her work a disservice if we put our best effort into lauding the poems written when that poise began to falter and her creative will lost control.

9

Geoffrey Hill

Geoffrey Hill's dense, formal, formidable poems have gradually established themselves, though he is still much less well known than he should be among ordinary readers of poetry. It is in the estimate of other poets that he stands particularly high – for example, in the answers to a 1972 questionnaire sent out by *The Review* to many poets and critics, the poet most often mentioned as a hopeful sign was Hill, specifically on the strength of his *Mercian Hymns* (1971). But *Mercian Hymns* – one of the finest achievements during the period with which this essay deals – did not appear from nowhere: its roots can be seen in *For the Unfallen* (1959) and *King Log* (1968).

Hill's deeply serious concerns and the ceremonial exactness of his language were already apparent in poems written before he was twenty – in 'Genesis', 'Holy Thursday' and 'God's Little Mountain':

> Below, the river scrambled like a goat
> Dislodging stones. The mountain stamped its foot,
> Shaking, as from a trance. And I was shut
> With wads of sound into a sudden quiet.
>
> ('God's Little Mountain')

These early poems, later collected in *For the Unfallen*, have an ample but severely controlled rhetoric which he continued to master. There is a rapt sense of struggle for exactness, for the precise word which will also be the resonant word: 'Where fish at dawn ignite the powdery lake'. *King Log* took the process much further, so that sometimes the taut compression becomes congestion, a tight-lipped ritualistic speech impressive in its gestures but not offering a ready key:

Geoffrey Hill
Elizabeth Cook

Anguish bloated by the replete scream.
Flesh of abnegation: the poem
Moves grudgingly to its extreme form,

Vulnerable, to the lamp's fierce head
Of well-trimmed light. In darkness outside,
Foxes and rain-sleeked stones and the dead –

Aliens of such a theme – endure
Until I could cry 'Death! Death!' as though
To exacerbate that suave power;

('Three Baroque Meditations')

The two substantial sequences in *King Log* – 'Funeral Music' and 'The Songbook of Sebastian Arrurruz' – show distinct contrasts both in theme and in the way Hill uses compressed and chiselled language. 'Funeral Music' consists of eight fourteen-line poems suggested by bloody incidents during the fifteenth-century Wars of the Roses: an attempt, as Hill has characteristically commented, at 'a florid grim music broken by grunts and shrieks':

> They bespoke doomsday and they meant it by
> God, their curved metal rimming the low ridge.
> But few appearances are like this. Once
> Every five hundred years a comet's
> Over-riding stillness might reveal men
> In such array, livid and featureless,
> With England crouched beastwise beneath it all.
> 'Oh, that old northern business . . .' A field
> After battle utters its own sound
> Which is like nothing on earth, but is earth.
> Blindly the questing snail, vulnerable
> Mole emerge, blindly we lie down, blindly
> Among carnage the most delicate souls
> Tup in their marriage-blood, gasping 'Jesus'.

The brooding sombreness of this is not simply pitying and elegiac: it is laced through with ironies, each phrase is delicately poised to re-create (without loose atmospherics or over-colourful images) a precise and horrible scene, of scrupulous interest in itself and beyond itself; a sound 'Which is like nothing on earth, but is earth'. In an early essay on Hill's work ('Cliche as "Responsible Speech"'), Christopher Ricks demonstrated the way in which Geoffrey Hill uses casual phrases and dead metaphors so that they are 'rinsed and restored', as 'like nothing on earth' is treated in the line just quoted. The 'grim music' of this sequence is orchestrated in this fashion, and the effect is both massive and finely sensitive.

'The Songbook of Sebastian Arrurruz' is a more
fragmentary and oblique group which 'represents the work of
an apocryphal Spanish poet' – a device which distances but
does not coldly objectify moods of regret and sexual desolation:
bitterness, loss, hopeless sensuality conflict:

> There would have been things to say, quietness
> That could feed on our lust, refreshed
> Trivia, the occurrences of the day;
> And at night my tongue in your furrow.
>
> Without you I am mocked by courtesies
> And chat, where satisfied women push
> Dutifully toward some unneeded guest
> Desirable features of conversation.
>
> ('From the Latin')★

But the poems are not just fictions about a former passion; they
are themselves embodiments of the strategies to which a poet is
forced when he grapples with his material and turns it into art,
finding how (as William Empson once put it) to 'learn a style
from a despair'.

The thirty prose poems that make up *Mercian Hymns* centre
on the eighth-century king of the West-Midlands, Offa, but the
effort here is not towards the re-creation of the past as it was
with 'Funeral Music'. The commanding and unifying figure
is sometimes the ancient king, sometimes the poet himself
in childhood or present manhood: throughout the sequence,
the remote past, the recent past and the present are obliquely
presented, often within the space of a single section – as is plain
from the beginning:

> King of the perennial holly-groves, the riven sand-
>   stone: overlord of the M5: architect of the his-

toric rampart and ditch, the citadel at Tamworth,
the summer hermitage in Holy Cross: guardian of
the Welsh Bridge and the Iron Bridge: contractor
to the desirable new estates: saltmaster: money-
changer: commissioner for oaths: martyrologist:
the friend of Charlemagne.

'I liked that,' said Offa, 'sing it again.'

('Mercian Hymns I')★

If *Mercian Hymns* has any stylistic source other than the historical
sources to which Hill's notes make droll and learned references,
it may be partly in St-John Perse's *Anabasis*, which T.S. Eliot
translated and published in 1931, and partly in David Jones (see
pp. 9–10); but really the method and tone are like nothing else
in English – complex, rich, many-layered, an intricately worked
meditation on history, tradition, order, power and memory,
in which the precision of the language and the mysterious
reverberations of the past combine to achieve something
completely inevitable and true:

'Now when King Offa was alive and dead', they were
all there, the funereal gleemen: papal legate and
rural dean; Merovingian car-dealers, Welsh mercen-
aries; a shuffle of house-carls.

He was defunct. They were perfunctory. The ceremony
stood acclaimed. The mob received memorial vouch-
ers and signs.

After that shadowy, thrashing midsummer hail-storm,
Earth lay for a while, the ghost-bride of livid
Thor, butcher of strawberries, and the shire-tree
dripped red in the arena of its uprooting.

('Mercian Hymns XXVII')★

Hill's book *Tenebrae* (1978) returned to the strict forms of his work before *Mercian Hymns*: the opening sequence, 'The Pentecost Castle', draws on old Spanish songs (*coplas*) of sacred and profane love, and others have their points of departure in German poems. But the main body of the book, made up of the sonnet-sequences 'Lachrimae' and 'An Apology for the Revival of Christian Architecture in England', relates much more to English devotional and meditative models, with a majestic reverberance that sometimes reminds one of Crashaw, sometimes of Tennyson, but so hammered and turned that they could be by no one but Hill:

> Autumn resumes the land, ruffles the woods
> with smoky wings, entangles them. Trees shine
> out from their leaves, rocks mildew to moss-green;
> the avenues are spread with brittle floods.
>
> Platonic England, house of solitudes,
> rests in its laurels and its injured stone,
> replete with complex fortunes that are gone,
> beset by dynasties of moods and clouds.
>
> It stands, as though at ease with its own world,
> the mannerly extortions, languid praise,
> all that devotion long since bought and sold,
>
> the rooms of cedar and soft-thudding baize,
> tremulous boudoirs where the crystals kissed
> in cabinets of amethyst and frost.

> ('The Laurel Axe': from 'An Apology for the
> Revival of Christian Architecture in England')*

Hill's *The Mystery of the Charity of Charles Peguy* (1983) is a long, allusive meditation, written in sonorous quatrains, on the implications of the life and death of the French poet, and it has been acutely called 'an oblique autobiography of the spirit'. And his *Collected Poems* (1985) gathers together everything that has appeared in book form, and adds the three part 'Hymns to Our Lady of Chartres'.

10

The 'Group' and after

One 'community of letters' that as early as the mid-1950s was taking notice of Ted Hughes, even before the publication of *The Hawk in the Rain*, was the so-called 'Group' – a loosely-organised assemblage of poets who (first in Cambridge under the chairmanship of Philip Hobsbaum, then – and more importantly – at Edward Lucie-Smith's house in London) met once a week to discuss one another's poems in an atmosphere of watchful sobriety, rigorously unsparing criticism, and to a less certain extent mutual esteem and emulation. The Group has long dispersed, but several of its members still show some of the characteristics (or bear the scars) of that formative critical workshop.

In a good essay on the Group, Roger Garfitt has written: 'As a cultural encounter, its effects have not yet terminated; as a cultural institution, there was a time-limit to its full effectiveness'. Edward Lucie-Smith, in his foreword to *A Group Anthology*, said: 'The only principle to which we would all subscribe is that poetry is discussable . . . that the process by which words work in poetry in something open to rational examination'. In a review of that book, Alvarez commented that there was a Group preoccupation: 'It is with, in one word, nastiness'. If there is a point at which these three observations meet, I have not found it, nor indeed is it very useful part-way through the 1990s to discuss as a phenomenon (other than in Garfitt's historical terms) the possible unity of a caravan that has passed on. I want instead to look at some of those who were once members.

Peter Porter is in many ways the most successful of them, and his range and confidence have greatly expanded. In his first book (*Once Bitten Twice Bitten*, 1961) he seemed primarily a satirist, a fierce neo-Jacobean demolisher of social aspirations, the rich, the smug, the phoney, 'the smoothies of our Elizabethan age'. It was exhilaratingly unpleasant, but already it looks a bit dated:

Peter Porter

> Cavalry-twilled tame publishers praising Logue,
> Classics Honours Men promoting Jazzetry,
>
> ('John Marston Advises Anger')

Such references will need footnotes before long. The satire
has continued in successive books, but gradually Porter has
emerged more solidly (and no less entertainingly) as an elegiac
poet, with a sardonic approach to death and the things of
the dead. He is a witty and exact namer of objects, and his
poems are dense with them; but the effect of this is not to turn
them into documentaries but fictions, so that they read like
discontinuous parts of a huge verse novel, a *roman fleuve* of our
time:

Ten thousand unemployed are rioting
The night your viola concerto's premièred.
The light of diamonds speaks to your pale wits.
'I saw the host that sat and heard the king
Speak to them on death. We will not be spared,
Our country's a cold whore, a Gräfenitz.'

The town's on fire. The bombers will return.
A priest brings round the late-night watered milk.
The asylum clock ticks plainly in the dark.
'This is the sermon. Until our bodies burn
God can't see us.' In your last silk
Shirt by bomb light you are fingering Bach.

('Steps on the Way')

Porter has said that from the beginning his poems 'have polarized about the art and life of the past and the everyday world of the present'. In his work the Holy Roman Empire, John Cage, Bach, the experimental-ridiculous, advertising slogans, Cluny, Carthage, Beverly Hills and the Black Country coexist, living parts of the continuous world of the imagination:

God is a Super-Director
who's terribly good at crowd scenes,
but He has only one tense, the present.
Think of pictures –
Florentine or Flemish, with Christ
or a saint – the softnesses of Luke,
skulls of Golgotha, craftsmen's
instruments of torture – everything is go!

('The Old Enemy')

Some of his most skilful work in this mingled area of past and present has been in his versions of Martial, the Roman poet of the first century AD. Porter has remodelled many of Martial's epigrams, freely using anachronism as a telescoping device in the cause of vividness and relevance:

It's good to have a quiver-full of kids, Cinna,
       even these days –
to hell with the population explosion,
your little woman's done a great job.
       There's just one matter I'd mention,
       none of them is yours!
Nor your neighbours', nor your friends',
nor the Elks', nor the Buffaloes', nor the Rotarians',
nor even an overnight hippy's in the sleep-out!
       You can tell this lot were mapped
       on unmade morning beds or sliding mats.
       Here's one with steel-wool hair;
       a gift from Santra the Cook;

                ('After Martial', VI xxxix)

Porter commands equally well mordantly colloquial inventions ('Your Attention Please', 'A Consumer's Report'), direct but more formal and sententious pieces ('Seahorses', 'Fossil Gathering'), and an exuberantly rough satirical mode, like a grinning death's-head, shown in 'Applause for Death':

He's given a thousand Oxford lectures
And named a score of noble Hectors
Who left the earth like Hemingway
Lighter in animals for their stay;
His policy of defoliation
Gave Concrete Poetry to the nation;

His critical triumphs are recorded
In the ten books Leavis lauded
And he'll be there at the wheelwright's shop
When modernity shuffles to a stop

This vein of satire is more playfully worked out in the second of his two 'Poems with French Titles' (from *Preaching to the Converted*, 1972), 'Mort aux Chats', an amusing essay in rhetoric – the rhetoric of prejudice and bigotry, whereby strong feelings are based on misinformation, ignorance, intolerance, fear and hatred:

I blame my headache and my
plants dying on to cats.
Our district is full of them,
property values are falling.
When I dream of God I see
a Massacre of Cats. Why
should they insist on their own
language and religion, who
needs to purr to make his point?
Death to all cats! The Rule
of Dogs shall last a thousand years!

('Mort aux Chats')

All Porter's books have this element of satire, but for some time his elegiac mode has been in the ascendant, particularly since *The Cost of Seriousness* (1978). Some of the most moving poems in it, and in its successor *English Subtitles* (1981), have their origin in the tragic early death of his wife. 'An Exequy', deliberately written in the same short-lined couplets as the famous elegy the seventeenth-century poet Henry King wrote for his own wife, is the most direct in its tone:

The rooms and days we wandered through
Shrink in my mind to one – there you
Lie quite absorbed by peace – the calm
Which life could not provide is balm
In death. Unseen by me, you look
Past bed and stairs and half-read book
Eternally upon your home,
The end of pain, the left alone.

('An Exequy')

But Porter's range of reference has by no means diminished: high art, rediscoveries of his native Australia (from which he moved to London in 1951), annotations of Italy and the changing face of Britain, are all fuel for his inventiveness and restless intelligence. The Group perhaps gave him confidence in his earlier days to develop, particularly in the direction of argumentative and even polemical poems; but for many years his peculiar genius has been self-propelled. His *Collected Poems* (1983) impressively gathered together almost everything he had published since the early 1960s.

Since the *Collected Poems*, Porter's fertile, erudite, dense and entertaining work has been added to in five further books. Their titles, and the titles of the poems within them, are as inventive and teasing as ever: *The Automatic Oracle*, *The Chair of Babel*, 'The Village Explainer', 'The Cheque is in the Post', 'On Mallarmé's Answer Machine', 'Porter's Retreat'. To his habitual (but never habit-ridden) intellectual gusto there has always been a melancholy side, a sense of doom; as 'we walk out in the cold and pathless air', however, there has usually been the acompaniment of something more bracing, and also playful.

Another prolific and inventive member of the Group, admired (as Garfitt put it) for 'his versatility and panache', was George MacBeth. Right from the beginning, in the poems he published while he was an Oxford undergraduate in the early and mid-1950s, there was an element of intellectual teasing in MacBeth, as if he deliberately courted an outraged or irritated response. This notion of provocative play was exemplified in such poems as 'Scissor-Man' and 'A True Story', through a great deal of *A Doomsday Book* (1965) – particularly in the 'poem-games', 'Fin du Globe' and 'The Ski Murders' – and was apparent throughout *The Orlando Poems* (1971), a sequence which seems to take the open-ended structure of Ted Hughes's *Crow* but produces light squibs rather than smouldering grenades.

There was a cheerful insolence about all this, but MacBeth's labelling of himself as 'the trapeze-artist of the abyss' was a typically ambiguous jest, toying with the genuine disturbances that seemed to underlie much of his poetry. When he was at his most autobiographical, in such earlier poems as 'The Miner's Helmet' and 'The Drawer', in such later poems as 'On the Death of May Street', and in the books that began with *Poems of Love and Death* (1980), there are few such extravagances. Something more sombre and more personally engaged began to show itself in particular with *Poems from Oby* (1982), an impressively unified book which drew almost entirely on his experience of the place in rural Norfolk to which he withdrew in 1979 after many years of living in London and abroad. Here he celebrated 'the luck of settlement, finding a piece of land to feel secure on, and someone to live there with'.

The almost Horatian sense of 'the good place', marking his feeling of purpose and stability in his second marriage (to the novelist Lisa St Aubin de Teran) and the birth of his first child, was widely recognised, in such poems as 'This Evening, Lisa':

> I walk tonight through silence, and watch smoke
> Circle above the chimneys of your aims
> In quiet air; and, hearing the far stroke
> Of human axes, I renounce cold games
>
> As my intent; and, by the sound of blades
> Through fallen wood, at distance, I defer
> To country ease.

But this idyll was short-lived. MacBeth's next book, *The Long Darkness* (1983), found as its main subject the terminal illness of his mother-in-law, to whom he was deeply attached. And soon after came the desertion of his wife and the collapse of the marriage, commemorated in the anguish of *Anatomy of a Divorce* (1988):

> Where were you last night?
> Don't answer, I
> Know where you were.
>
> What was his name?
> Don't answer, I
> Know his name.
>
> No, I don't want to know
> Who you weren't with. When
> I say you were
> With someone, that's where you were.
>
> Pass me the tongs.
>
> ('The Inquisition')

There was a brief happier interlude, with his final marriage and his departure with his new wife to Galway in the West of Ireland, and this can be seen in *Trespassing* (1991), a book which responded to his new home with a sense of the monstrosities of Anglo-Irish history, though often with MacBeth's characteristic grotesque humour. But very soon came the first signs of the malignant motor-neurone disease which, painfully, memorably, and almost until the moment of his death, he unflinchingly recorded in his final book, *The Patient* (1992). The nakedness of these poems, particularly in a group of sonnets, is like nothing else in contemporary poetry. There is no games-playing here:

> Some days I do feel better. Then I know
> It couldn't come to this, it never would.

I'm much the same as I was long ago
When I could walk two thousand yards, and stand

Upright at parties, chatting. When the men
At petrol stations understood
The words I mouthed. Now is the same as then.
It isn't, though. These are the days when food

Falls from my grip, drink chokes me in my throat
And I'm a nervous nuisance, prone to tears.
The time has come when I put on my coat
With fumbling fingers, grappling with my fears

Of God knows what. Well, I know one that's worse
Than all the rest. My wife's become my nurse.

('The Worst Fear')*

George MacBeth's last collected volume, *Collected Poems 1958–1982* (1989), is probably the book which will most fully and accurately continue his reputation; but it should be augmented with *Anatomy of a Divorce*, *Trespassing*, and most certainly *The Patient*, before one can properly see his achievement. Not only his contemporaries but younger poets, too, remember him with firm affection: Carol Ann Duffy, for example, has written of him as 'justly regarded as one of our most inventive poets'.

Peter Redgrove studied science at Cambridge, and behind a good deal of his work there is the sense of a passionate scientist, someone who understands the physical laws of the universe but who at the same time sees them as a kind of magic. Redgrove has an imaginative richness which sometimes looks wildly eccentric, mystical and comic at once. Some of his poems seem to hold an enormous magnifying glass up to Nature, so that the uprooting of a daisy appears a labour of the same magnitude as the felling of a mighty oak; they can boil with an energy that is too muscle-bound:

I sit in the hot room and I sweat

And those wet red blooms like sliced tomatoes –

I want to get in there with a thick insulting stick

In his earlier work, Redgrove was seen to be something of the same sort of writer as Ted Hughes; but though both Hughes and Redgrove are possibly romantic soothsayers, and though their inspiration can often be seen as basically irrational – in fact basically *anti*-rational – Redgrove has become a more careful organiser of language than Hughes, at least in his more recent manifestations. The early prose-poem monologues, such as 'Mr Waterman' and 'The Sermon', were successful grotesque inventions which had an imposed dramatic form. More recent poems, such as 'The Idea of Entropy at Maenporth Beach', have a beautifully intense gracefulness mixed with the grotesquerie:

She laughs aloud, and bares her teeth again, and cries:
Now that I am all black, and running in my richness . . .
And knowing it a little, I shall take great care
To keep a little black about me somewhere.
A snotty nostril, a mourning nail will do.
Mud is a good dress, but not the best.
Ah, watch, she runs into the sea. She walks
In streaky white on dazzling sands that stretch
Like the whole world's pursy mud quite purged.

('The Idea of Entropy at Maenporth Beach')

Redgrove, over the years, has poured out so many books – not only of poems, but novels, stories, plays for radio and television, and such delvings into psycho-physiology as *The Wise Wound*, written in collaboration with his wife, Penelope Shuttle, herself a poet who shares almost all his concerns – that one can be bewildered by the range of his matters and manners. And yet it has been rightly said that he is never arbitrary, however much his polemical outbursts now and then have pushed him into the position of being an unacceptable Ted Hughes – warlock, shaman, going on crazily about menstruation rather than the recognisably rural (and therefore comfortable) Moortown.

His selected volume *The Moon Disposes: Poems 1954–1987* (1987) is a handy way of coming to terms with him. It shows an admirable consistency, and also the whole range of Redgrove's endlessly proliferating tones – intently observant, erotic, magical, violent, tender, humorous. Even if one simply dips into his most recent collection, *My Father's Trapdoors* (1994), the flavour is immediately recognisable. It is typically full of wild fancyings – explosive metamorphoses of central heating, fish, alcohol, Cornish seaports, even Staines Waterworks. In his poetic crucible – still part of the equipment of the Cambridge natural scientist – there is often a surprising retort, conjuring up tasty tricks from chemistry, mind-bending consequences from physics, alchemy from entomology, as in 'At the Butterfly Farm':

The bushes under the glass roof
In no breeze flutter with the butterflies
Whose gut-vaults are packed with fermenting plum juice,
With the molasses of bananas,
The cellars full of cells in which the soul feasts,

In which the spirit carouses the plum alcohols,
The banana brandies, and translates these joys

Into wobbly flights of magnificent oily garments.

Some of Alan Brownjohn's poems, such as 'Snow in Bromley' and 'We are going to see the rabbit' (from *The Railings*, 1961) became small classics of social comment, but his has been a very gradually achieved reputation. *Warrior's Career*, published in 1972 when he was forty, was the first really to show his range of techniques and sympathies, in particular in some cross-sections of invented human relationships. Brownjohn himself has said that a number of his poems tend towards 'the condition of fiction', almost as situations or incidents from a novel or short story: characters are revealed obliquely or through their own monologues – a girl disc-jockey, a smart young executive, salesmen and antique-dealers and politicians. There were many of these in *A Song of Good Life* (1975) and more again in *A Night in the Gazebo* (1980). Some are light, such as 'Especially' and the group of poems centring on a character called 'The Old Fox', an ingenious rogue; but most show a mingling of acute human observation with a basic melancholy, so that even the ridiculous or the reprehensible (as in the hotel managers in the title-poem of *A Night in the Gazebo*) are touched with sadness:

> Lastly, gaze out there at the crematorium.
>   Having consumed fourteen
> Tequilas in half-an-hour, a manager
> Is being consumed to rest. His wife comes first,
> And behind her follow forty-six girls in all,
> The youngest sixteen, the oldest thirty-four,
> And all in states of nostalgia or raw distress
> According to how lately they knew the man.
> So wife and girls compassionate each other
> As the clergyman, noting an ancient English
> Ritual of mourning, shakes each girl by the hand.
> If this can happen, the world must be good. It is ten
>   forty-five.

If there seems in Brownjohn to be a mildness of approach, a sidling-up to subjects rather than a confrontation with them, it might be a corrective to notice his own answer to the question 'What would you have us say about the poems?':

> I should like people to read my work and think it was like drinking lemonade, only to find a little later that it was

81

strongly laced. I'd want it to go down like lemonade but to hit them like vodka.

Increasingly, one of Brownjohn's tactics is to achieve his effects by working through narrative or anecdotal sequences, furnished with 'characters' – not so much the self-revealed types of his earlier work as the intermeshed participants in a particular world. An example of this is 'The Automatic Days' (in *The Observation Car*, 1990), a group of poems about the employees in a department store. But he is equally adept at inventing wittily satirical observations on human duplicity and human foibles which belong partly in the 'real', social world and partly in a wildly hysterical place, as in 'Bastard':

Into a suddenly sunny spring dawn
A bastard creeps out through a crack in some
Until-then immaculate-looking woodwork.

He inhales the air and smiles, and everything
Looks good to him. And so he take a few
Experimental paces, trying out

His legs and wondering what clothes to wear . . .

Because he plans to walk into an Organisation,
To stir things up inside an Organisation.
He is going to Go For It and get others Going,

And he's past Reception already, and up
In an express lift to a penthouse suite already,
And they have an office waiting for him already,

And his first dictated letters on a screen.

Such Brownjohn poems work cumulatively, building up to outrageous and hilarious climaxes. He is often surprising and subversive, sharply so.

Edwin Brock is another poet of social comment; he too was an attender of the Group, though he is not represented in *A Group Anthology*. His ironies are usually more straightforwardly presented than Brownjohn's, and they make neatly devastating points about violence and heartlessness: for example, two of his best-known poems, 'Five Ways to Kill a Man' and 'Song of the Battery Hen'. This second title became the title of his 'Selected Poems 1959–1975':

We can't grumble about accommodation:
we have a new concrete floor that's
always dry, four walls that are
painted white, and a sheet-iron roof
the rain drums on. A fan blows warm air
beneath our feet to disperse the smell
of chickenshit and, on dull days,
fluorescent lighting sees us.

('Song of the Battery Hen')

Through a great deal of Brock's work runs a common thread of supple, sometimes apparently artless but always direct and colloquial examination and self-examination. The manner is doggedly honest, touched with humorous self-deprecation:

These are my credentials:
I am clever
and I am aware.

You buy me
in a small transparent ball
almost entirely filled with water.

You shake me
and a plastic snowstorm
will ensue.

('A Man of the World')

The later poems, often concerned with both the loving intimacy and the precariousness of family life, use natural imagery – rivers, trees, cows, herons – as a counterpoint to what is actually an urban, as well as urbane, sense of poise. Nothing can quite banish his disquiet:

Truly these trees twist us with a hint
. of roots. I do not understand why
a concern for others is our responsibility
or God's. Only this is planned:
that we will grow vegetables, watching
week by week the soil reveal its hand.
That, and our rotting compost heap.

('These Trees')

11

Scotland and Wales

Despite the fact of ease of communication in Britain today – or perhaps partly because of it – there are certain regions that seem very conscious of themselves as entities: the role played by Liverpool and the North-East in the pop movement was significant. But the Celtic awareness in Scotland, Wales and Ireland has become even stronger during the present century, heightened in Ulster by the clash – the physical clash – between separate cultures. The expression of this has been mainly political, but there have been signs in the poetry of these countries too.

Ireland has been the most obvious case, and that requires another section in this survey. But even in the 1990s there have been passionate – and passionately articulated – manifestations of separateness in Scotland and in Wales. Introductions to recent anthologies of verse from these countries give one texts by which to argue what might be true here, what merely contentious; and, when Scottish and Welsh poets are enlisted into 'British' anthologies, and when these poets appear to take their own stand on their own ground, there is cause for reflection.

The so-called Scottish Renaissance has looked to the poet Hugh MacDiarmid at least as far back as the 1920s. MacDiarmid died in 1978, but his is still a potent and influential force, especially among those who have chosen to write in Lallans, the mixed literary-colloquial Scottish idiom which MacDiarmid did so much to promote. His first collection, *Sangschaw*, appeared in 1925, followed by *A Drunk Man Looks at the Thistle* and *Penny Wheep* the next year. These were campaigning books, but they made little impact beyond Scotland. It was not until MacDiarmid fiercely took the battle not just beyond language but beyond consensus politics that a wider world began to take notice; and by then it was too late – because MacDiarmid had ventured beyond nationalism towards eccentricity, even perverseness, so that the English could ignore him. And this they did, except to take note of his dogmatic foolishness, embracing – and between times rejecting – Communism, Scottish Nationalism, and putting on a clamour of posturings and stances so extreme and eccentric that no one outside Scotland could be expected to take any of it seriously.

Yet MacDiarmid, however rebarbative his stance and his voice, his aggressiveness and his apparent attitudinising (rejoining the Communist Party at the moment the Soviet Army invaded Hungary in 1956, for example), must be taken seriously, if one is to understand the new Scottish poetry which followed him. Lallans (or what Douglas Dunn calls 'synthetic Scots') was for MacDiarmid part of a larger struggle, an international struggle, which went well beyond local linguistic skirmishes (Scottish *versus* 'standard' English) to confront much larger – and, one could say, often much cloudier – issues, such as an international philology. That way, often, madness lies; and MacDiarmid's later work, much of the time, looks to me like a prosy and sprawling attempt to say everything in a language which has no controls whatsoever. Yet no recent Scottish poet has quite been able to reject MacDiarmid.

It is a strange business, at least for the outsider. First, there followed a generation after MacDiarmid which took some of his early practices and precepts, and made them work: Sydney Goodsir Smith produced lyrics (many of them collected in Smith's *Collected Poems*, 1975) which are as attractive, in their dutiful Lallans way, as his master's. Robert Garioch (who died in 1980) was a comic observer of the Scottish scene, with a marvellous ear for the raciness of its speech:

> Last nicht in Scotland Street I met a man
> that gruppit my lapel – a kinna foreign
> cratur he seemed; he tellt me, There's a war on
> atween the Lang-nebs and the Big-heid Clan.
>
> I wasna fasht, I took him for a moron,
> naething byordnar, but he said, Ye're wan
> of thae lang-nebbit folk, and if I can,
> I'm gaunnae pash ye doun and rype your sporran.

> ('I'm Neutral')

Yet, for the outsider, the best poetry written in Scotland
for many years was not of this sort at all. It was a poetry
written by Norman MacCaig, Iain Crichton Smith, George
Mackay Brown – in English, without lexical oddities, and yet
from a standpoint which was clearly, unashamedly Scottish.
Lallans was not even a point at issue; Gaelic, the native Gaelic
language, is one of Iain Crichton Smith's possible tongues, but
it never obtruded into his English poems; and, as for Scottish
nationalism, it seemed as foreign as Welsh Nationalism had
quotably been for Dylan Thomas ('I only ever heard him
mention Welsh Nationalism once: he used three words, two of
them being "Welsh Nationalism"').

That witty standoffishness has been Norman MacCaig's
position from early on. Now, in his eighties, MacCaig can look
back on a lifetime of elegant, polished, exact dandification,
untroubled by nationalist incursions: he has reached a position
which cannot be assailed by such things. For the past several
decades, his poems have tended to be light and charming
perceptions, written in a relaxed free verse, rather than the
trim and trussed rhymed pieces with which he first made
his reputation in the 1950s. A recent example is 'London to
Edinburgh'*:

I'm waiting for the moment
when the train crosses the Border
and home creeps closer
at seventy miles an hour.

I dismiss the last four days
and their friendly strangers
into the past
that grows bigger every minute.

The train sounds urgent as I am,
it says home and home and home.
I light a cigarette
and sit smiling in the corner.

Scotland, I rush towards you
into my future that,
every minute,
grows smaller and smaller.

This genial openness is there in abundance, in poem after poem.
What has been missing for a long time is the witty precision
of form which can be found in such early MacCaig poems as
'Sheep Dipping':

They haul themselves ashore. With outraged cries
They waterfall uphill, spread out and stand
Dribbling salt water into flowers' eyes.

As I have said, Iain Crichton Smith has written in Gaelic as
well as in English, but his English poetry has no obvious verbal
relationship with anything Scottish. His settings and themes,
however, have much to do with Scotland, especially its remote
islands and highlands:

if I shall say I had a jar it would
be a black mountain in the Hebrides

and round it fly your blackbirds black as pitch
and in their centre with a holy book

a woman all in black reading the world
consisting of black crows in a black field.

('The Black Jar')

But the starkness of this poem is not typical of Smith, who is
a shapely writer in received forms, as in 'Dunoon and the Holy
Loch', in which the neat turns of rhyme ironically underline the scene:

The huge sea widens from us, mile on mile.
Kenneth MacKellar sings from the domed pier.
A tinker plays a ragged tune
on ragged pipes. He tramps under a moon
which rises like the dollar. Think how here
missiles like sugar rocks are all incised
with Alabaman Homer. These defend
the clattering tills, the taxis, thin pale girls
who wear at evening their Woolworth pearls
and from dewed railings gaze at the world's end.

And Smith also has an entertaining satirical side, for example in his five-part 'Chinese Poem', in which he adopts something of the tone of Arthur Waley's translations:

To Seumas Macdonald,
                     now resident in Edinburgh –
I am alone here, sacked from the Department
for alcoholic practices and disrespect.
A cold wind blows from Ben Cruachan.
There is nothing here but sheep and large boulders.
Do you remember the nights with *Reliquae Celticae*
and those odd translations by Calder?
Buzzards rest on the wires. There are many seagulls.
My trousers grow used to the dung.
What news from the frontier? Is Donald still Colonel?
Are there more pupils than teachers in Scotland?
I send you this by a small boy with a pointed head.
Don't trust him. He is a Campbell.

George Mackay Brown writes almost exclusively about his native Orkney, cold, rocky, depopulated, a place of shepherds, fishermen, and memories of the distant Norse past of feud and destruction. To this place and these matters, more to do with Scandinavia than Scottishness, Brown gives his grave and minute attention:

A silent conquering army,
The island dead,
Column on column, each with a stone banner
Raised over his head.

A green wave full of fish
Drifted far
In wavering westering ebb-drawn shoals beyond
Sinker or star.

A labyrinth of celled
And waxen pain.
Yet I come to the honeycomb often, to sip the finished
Fragrance of men.

('Kirkyard')★

Seven scythes leaned at the wall.
Beard upon golden beard
The last barley load
Swayed through the yard.
The girls uncorked the ale.
Fiddle and feet moved together.
Then between stubble and heather
A horseman rode.

('Taxman')★

The 'New Generation' promotion recently showed a new wave of young Scottish poets. Behind some of them lies the comic-demotic of Tom Leonard and Liz Lochhead, of whom George Mackay Brown commented: 'She is a truly modern poet in that she writes – I almost wrote, *speaks* – in the very tone and accent and rhymes of the 1980s'. But perhaps the most influential figure, in his range and variety, has been Edwin Morgan. Morgan did not properly begin to make his mark until he was in his late forties, with the publication of *The Second Life* (1968), a book which showed international, experimental, modernist tendencies, and an exuberant (and sometimes garrulous) sense of humour. He has also been an inventive and witty maker of miniatures, as in his 'Chinese Cat'*:

```
p m r k g n i a o u
p m r k g n i a o
p m r k n i a o
p m r n i a o
p m r i a o
p m i a o
m i a o
m a o
```

Another takes a famous poem by the seventeenth-century Japanese poet Basho and turns it into a 'Summer Haiku'*:

```
    Pool.
  Pe opl
    e  plop!
    Cool.
```

But Morgan's chief Scottish legacy can be seen in such sequences as his 'Glasgow Sonnets' and 'Sonnets from Scotland', which confidently blend close observation, historical and political concerns, and a discriminating lexical breadth which is equally at home with Scottish words and much more exotic language:

> A shilpit dog fucks grimly by the close.
> Late shadows lengthen slowly, slogans fade.
> The YY PARTICK TOI grins from its shade
> like the last strains of some lost *libera nos*
> *a malo*. No deliverer ever rose
> from these stone tombs to get the hell they made
> unmade.

> (from 'Glasgow Sonnets' II)

Among the young poets in Scotland, Robert Crawford and W.N. Herbert have learned from Morgan's example. But there are wilder and freer spirits too, among them Kathleen Jamie, the title-poem of whose collection *The Way We Live* (1987) is an exultant hymn to risk-taking unhindered by boundaries:

> Pass the tambourine, let me bash out praises
> to the Lord God of movement, to Absolute
> non-friction, flight, and the scarey side:
> death by avalanche, birth by failed contraception.
> Of chicken tandoori and reggae, loud, from tenements,
> commitment, driving fast and unswerving
> friendship. Of tee-shirts on pulleys, giros and Bombay,
> barmen, dreaming waitresses with many fake-gold
> bangles. Of airports, impulse, and waking to uncertainty,
> to strip-lights, motorways, or that pantheon –
> the mountains.

> ('The way we live')

Other poets who are Scottish, or who have been considered Scottish because of birth or background, are dealt with elsewhere in this essay: George MacBeth, Douglas Dunn, Carol Ann Duffy. Indeed, significant areas of MacBeth's and Dunn's work have been self-consciously Scottish, but their first reputations were made on other grounds, which is why they do not appear in this section.

Though, of the living Celtic languages, Welsh is far more widely used, in speech and in print, than its related languages in Ireland or Scotland, so that there is still a living tradition of Welsh poets writing in Welsh, the so-called Anglo-Welsh scene seems to have had less impact on the world outside. There has been an impressive twentieth-century ancestry (David Jones, Dylan Thomas, Vernon Watkins, Alun Lewis), but for several years the most generally known of Welsh poets writing in English have been simply two: R.S. Thomas and Dannie Abse.

There are considerable contrasts between these two, in almost every possible way, except for the Welshness they have in common. Thomas, though he writes poems only in English, learnt Welsh as a young man during his training as a clergyman in the Church in Wales, has spent almost his whole life in remote rural places, and has increasingly become a fervent Welsh Nationalist. Abse's background is urban, and he has spent most of his life away from Wales, working as a doctor in London. He is consciously Jewish, just as he is consciously Welsh, but the personality that comes through his writing is genial, generous, liberal, not looking for either religious or political confrontation.

Thomas's earlier poems, for the first twenty years or so (he published his first slim volume at his own expense as long ago as 1946), are hauntingly evocative portraits of the people and landscapes of depopulated hills and valleys in Wales, such as 'Iago Prytherch' and 'Cynddylan on a Tractor'. These had certainly established his reputation by the late 1950s. Then, in the late 1960s, the preoccupations began to change. Now Thomas began to take on the big problem of God, not confined to narrow acres or to Wales, but faced as someone, or something, who was probably universal, possibly non-existent, endlessly to be sought, yearned for, questioned, argued with, maybe settled for, never quite rejected even at moments when he, or it, seemed to have absconded:

R.S. Thomas

                For some
    it is all darkness: for me, too,
    it is dark. But there are hands
    there I can take, voices to hear
    solider than the echoes
    without. And sometimes a strange light
    shines, purer than the moon,
    casting no shadow, that is
    the halo upon the bones
    of the pioneers who died for truth.

                        ('Groping')

Thomas is not a poet to be quoted effectively in odd lines or blinding phrases; he works his way through an observation, a situation or a conundrum with a bleak wholeness. In what he has called his 'linguistic confrontation with ultimate reality', he has more and more come to a language and a form both very plain and challengingly intense. On the page, the breaks between the lines may seem to have no significance; but read aloud, they are certainly not prose:

I have seen the sun break through
to illuminate a small field
for a while, and gone my way
and forgotten it. But that was the pearl
of great price, the one field that had
the treasure in it. I realize now
that I must give all that I have
to possess it. Life is not hurrying

on to a receding future, nor hankering after
an imagined past. It is the turning
aside like Moses to the miracle
of the lit bush, to a brightness
that seemed as transitory as your youth
once, but is the eternity that awaits you.

('The Bright Field')*

Dannie Abse's warm, humane, sometimes untidily cluttered poems are quite different from Thomas's austere and laconic grapplings with 'ultimate reality'. He mildly acknowledges, with humour, that his poems mostly ignore any traditional close attention to Nature ('As I Was Saying') or animals ('Florida'), and his thoughts about the transcendental or spiritual tend to be either deliberately flippant ('Even') or teasing ('The Power of Prayer'); and when he confronts such matters more directly, as in 'The Abandoned', he can seem evasive.

Abse's real strengths come from his patiently recalled, totally unexploitative lifetime as a practising doctor. Here he has an exactness and an authority which can be tellingly anecdotal:

'Most Welshmen are worthless,
an inferior breed, doctor.'
He did not know I was Welsh.
Then he praised the architects
of the German death-camps –
did not know I was a Jew.
He called liberals, 'White blacks',
and continued to invent curses.

When I palpated his liver
I felt the soft liver of Goering;
when I lifted my stethoscope
I heard the heartbeats of Himmler;
when I read his encephalograph
I thought, 'Sieg heil, mein Führer'.

In the clinic's dispensary
red berry of black bryony,
cowbane, deadly nightshade, deathcap.
Yet I prescribed for him
as if he were my brother.

Later that night I must have slept
on my arm: momentarily
my right hand lost its cunning.

('Case history')★

And in 'The Stethoscope', he ventures into a metaphysical world which he earns the right to explore:

Through it,
over young women's tense abdomens,
I have heard the sound of creation
and, in a dead man's chest, the silence
before creation began.

12

Ireland: North and South

Seamus Heaney has been noticed and celebrated ever since
his first book, *Death of a Naturalist*, was published in 1966,
when he was twenty-six. That book was praised for its
sensuous freshness, its strong taste of the physical details
that clustered round Heaney's memories of his childhood
in rural Derry. To the British (or perhaps more accurately
one should say 'to the British and Northern Irish'), who
have for many years been largely an urban people but who
have keen yearnings for 'the country', Heaney's poems gave
new impetus to nostalgias associated with Wordsworth,
Hardy and Edward Thomas, and also seemed to relate
to such works as Laurie Lee's best-selling evocation of
his own rural Gloucestershire childhood, *Cider with Rosie*.
Bulls, wells, milking, digging, frogspawn, blackberries, the
poignant reek of dung and clay, were efficiently recorded and
transmitted:

> As a child, they could not keep me from wells
> And old pumps with buckets and windlasses.
> I loved the dark drop, the trapped sky, the smells
> Of waterweed, fungus and dank moss.

('Personal Helicon')

With *Door into the Dark* (1969) Heaney began to move beyond
himself, looking for example at 'the mysterious life-cyle of the
eel and the compulsive work-cycles in the eel-fisherman's life' in
'A Lough Neagh Sequence'. In *Wintering Out* (1972) he began to
make a journey he was to repeat, back into the remote past, of
Ireland and of prehistoric man:

Seamus Heaney
Caroline Forbes

We picked flints,
Pale and dirt-veined,

So small finger and thumb
Ached around them;

Cold beads of history and home
We fingered, a cave-mouth flame

Of leaf and stick
Trembling at the mind's wick.

('Tinder')

All these manoeuvres, both of extending his subject-matter beyond rural simplicities and of tightening up his style so that it became an economical and refined reduction to essentials, reached their maturity in *North* (1975). By the time it was published, the renewed 'troubles' of Northern Ireland had been going on for over five years; and as the tension and violence increased, dominating the headlines and polarising the province, and as Heaney's reputation had grown, there was evident pressure on him to 'say something', to speak out. But in spite of his upbringing as a member of the Roman Catholic minority (family, church, education, expectations), he was not, and is not, deeply political or conspicuously partisan. In a poem included in *North*, 'Freedman', he suggested, ironically, that he had been liberated by his education, 'manumitted' from serfdom by his ability to pass exams and become a poet:

And poetry wiped my brow and sped me.
Now they will say I bite the hand that fed me.

He knew where he came from, he was skilled in historical knowledge. The perspectives of history, especially remote history, extended in his poems, so that many of them followed a method of delicate archaeological probing, into language as much as into 'remains'.

North was immediately recognised as a triumph. It included poems that were colloquial, even anecdotal, relaxed and yet sharp, such as 'Freedman', 'Whatever You Say Say Nothing' and the group under the overall title 'Singing School'. Most impressively, its meditations on the Iron Age corpses exhumed from a Danish bog in the 1950s and the whole inheritance of violent retribution, were handled with ratpness, with imaginative density and with gracefully accurate precision. In 'Punishment', the execution of an Iron Age girl for adultery is seen as analogous to the ritualistic punishment of women, presumed traitors, in Northern Ireland, who have been shaved and tarred by extremists as an 'example' to others. The poet is torn between the force of 'connive' and the force of 'understand':

My poor scapegoat,

I almost love you
but would have cast, I know,
the stones of silence.
I am the artful voyeur

of your brain's exposed
and darkened combs,
your muscles' webbing
and all your numbered bones:

I who have stood dumb
when your betraying sisters,
cauled in tar,
wept by the railings,

who would connive
in civilized outrage
yet understand the exact
and tribal, intimate revenge.

('Punishment')

Such continuities, whether grim as in 'Punishment' or benign
as in many other poems, are important to Heaney. For four
years in the 1970s, Heaney and his family withdrew to a cottage
in deep countryside in Co. Wicklow, and his next three books
(beginning with *Field Work*, 1979) show much burrowing
back into notions of craft, ceremony, eternal recurrence. With
his book *Seeing Things* (1991), at one level we seem to be
back in the world first recorded in *Death of a Naturalist*, in
summonings-up of precise moments of his childhood: playing
football, fishing, remembering his father with his ashplant, his
pitchfork, spraying potatoes, pegging out string in the garden.

But there are differences. One difference between early
Heaney and late Heaney is that the poet now seems more
deliberately, more solemnly, to acknowledge that his craft (never
doubted) should be open to, and enlarged by, 'vision'. It aims to
illuminate:

Heaviness of being. And poetry
Sluggish in the doldrums of what happens.
Me waiting until I was nearly fifty
To credit marvels. Like the tree-clock of tin cans
The tinkers made. So long for air to brighten,
Time to be dazzled and the heart to lighten.

('Fosterling')

Seeing Things, indeed, begins and ends with visions, but they are
not directly Heaney's: his translations of part of Virgil's *Aeneid*
and part of Dante's *Inferno*. They are there with a purpose –
as other ways of invoking his dead father, celebrated more
mundanely and personally elsewhere in the book.

Heaney's reputation, in the United States as well as in
Britain, is now very high. Deserved though this is, an almost
inevitable concomitant has been that other gifted poets from
the province have had rather less attention. Nevertheless,
four of them (two contemporaries of Heaney's, two rather
younger) have been much noticed. These are Michael Longley,
Derek Mahon, Tom Paulin and Paul Muldoon.

Michael Longley was a contemporary and friend of
Heaney's at university in Belfast. He has said of himself that
from the beginning he has 'been preoccupied with form –
pushing a shape as far as it will go, exploring its capacities to
control and its tendencies to disintegrate'. In the early 1970s he
wrote some verse letters, including ones to his Roman Catholic
friend Heaney and to his fellow Protestant Derek Mahon, which
express with tight control and sinewy intelligence the conflicts
of their embattled Northern Irish homeland. In his letter to
Heaney, Longley recollects 'the old stories':

The midden of cracked hurley sticks
Tied to recall the crucifix,
Of broken bones and lost scruples,
The blackened hearth, the blazing gable's
Telltale cinder where we may

Scorch our shins until that day
We sleepwalk through a No Man's Land
Lipreading to an Orange band.

('Letter to Seamus Heaney')

And in a companion letter to Mahon:

And did we come into our own
When, minus muse and lexicon,
We traced in August sixty-nine
Our imaginary Peace Line
Around the burnt-out houses of
The Catholics we'd scarcely loved,
Two Sisyphuses come to budge
The sticks and stones of an old grudge,

Two poetic conservatives
In the city of guns and long knives,
Our ears receiving then and there
The stereophonic nightmare
Of the Shankhill and the Falls,
Our matches struck on crumbling walls
To light us as we moved at last
Through the back alleys of Belfast?

('Letter to Derek Mahon')

But Longley is certainly not primarily a political poet. The
burden of many of his poems is the inter-penetration of things,
the responsibility of one thing for another, as in 'Self-portrait', a
truly witty poem which ends:

I am, you will have noticed, all fingers and thumbs
But, then, so is the wing of a bat, a bird's wing.
I articulate through the nightingale's throat,
Sing with the vocal chords of the orang-outang.

With exactness and elegance, he establishes moments of personal
vision, strangely and tenderly:

I gaze at myself before I was born. A shadow
Against her liver and spine I share her body
With my brother's body, two skulls in a basket,
Two sets of bones that show no abnormalities.
I want her to eat the world, giblets, marrow,
Tripes and offal, fish, birds, fields of grain.
But because it is April nineteen thirty-nine
I should look up to the breasts that will weep for me
And prescribe in the dark a salad of landcress,
Fennel like hair, the sky-blue of borage flowers.

('X-Ray')*

Longley's *Gorse Fires* (1991) triumphantly draws together
his many fine qualities, and indeed that book at last began to
bring him his due recognition, so that now he is widely seen
as just as assured and excellent a writer as Heaney. Longley's
relaxed, casual, but also poignant humour is delightful in
'Detour'*:

I want my funeral to include this detour
Down the single street of a small market town,
On either side of the procession such names
As Philbin, O'Malley, MacNamara, Keane.
A reverent pause to let a herd of milkers pass

Will bring me face to face with grubby parsnips,
Cauliflowers that glitter after a sunshower,
Then hay rakes, broom handles, gas cylinders.
Reflected in the slow sequence of shop windows
I shall be part of the action when his wife
Draining the potatoes into a steamy sink
Calls to the butcher to get ready for dinner
And the publican descends to change a barrel.
From behind the one locked door for miles around
I shall prolong a detailed conversation
With the man in the concrete telephone kiosk
About where my funeral might be going next.

Derek Mahon's is a more markedly ironical, dandified,
referential, indeed literary talent, casually allusive, as in 'Rage
for Order', which transplants Wallace Stevens to contemporary
Northern Ireland:

Somewhere beyond the scorched gable end and the
    burnt-out buses
there is a poet indulging
    his wretched rage for order –
or not as the case may be; for his
        is a dying art,
        an eddy of semantic scruples
        in an unstructurable sea.

Mahon has often proclaimed his allegiance to Louis MacNeice,
who has given him licence and authority to use a wide
range of manners and modes (from Basho to Beckett) in
exploring his sceptical and gloomy sense of doom and exile:
for much of his life he has been away from Ireland. His
Selected Poems (1991) begin with an elegy for MacNeice ('In
Carrowdore Churchyard') and end with one for Camus. The

most impressive poem in the book is a meditation with the bleak title 'A Disused Shed in Co. Wexford', which has become Mahon's most generally admired piece. Here 'A thousand mushrooms crowd to a keyhole', and are celebrated as dumb survivors whose tenacity spells out a hard-won lesson:

> They are begging us, you see, in their wordless way,
> To do something, to speak on their behalf
> Or at least not to close the door again.
> Lost people of Treblinka and Pompeii!
> 'Save us, save us', they seem to say,
> 'Let the god not abandon us
> Who have come so far in darkness and in pain.
> We too had our lives to live.
> You with your light meter and relaxed itinerary,
> Let not our naive labours have been in vain!'

In Heaney, Longley and Mahon, political concerns, though intermittently and sometimes mutedly present in their poems, are not central. For Tom Paulin they have increasingly become so; and yet he has spent less of his life in the Ireland that obsesses him than any of the others. Paulin's politics doggedly and sometimes ferociously take on what he has called with deliberation (in a prose pamphlet) 'Ireland and the English Crisis'. His earlier poems were often dour and yet lyrically subdued urban landscapes:

> The state's centre terrifies, its frontiers
> Are sealed against its enemies. Shouts echo
> Through the streets of this angry polity
>> Whose waters might be kind.
>
> Its justice is bare wood and limewashed bricks,
> Institutional fixtures, uniforms,
> The shadows of watchtowers on public squares,
>> A hemp noose over a greased trap.
>
>>> ('A Just State')

Paul Muldoon
Niall McDairmid

His third book, *Liberty Tree* (1983) began to show more oblique
manoeuvres: indignation and disgust are there, but also a
metaphorical freedom:

> Masculine Islam, the rule of the Just,
> Egyptian sand dunes and geometry,
> A theology of rifle-butts and executions:
> These are the places where the spirit dies.
> And now, in Desertmartin's sandy light,
> I see a culture of twigs and bird-shit
> Waving a gaudy flag it loves and curses.

('Desertmartin')

There began, too, a free and sometimes freakish use of Ulster
dialect, aggressively challenging supposed 'English' decorum:

Here's a wet sheugh
smells like a used sheath,
and here's frogspawn
and a car battery
under a screggy hawthorn.
They're having a geg
chucking *weebits* and *yuk*
and laughing at the blups –

('S/He')

These scathing, laconic, often obscure annotations of Ireland are
part of a polemical programme which continues and extends
to other concerns: Paulin's dialectics often dig into dialect to
establish a language – both rough and sophisticated – which
worries away at sex-war as well as class-war and sectarian war.
Paulin's is a vexed, gritty, impatient, sometimes choked and
incoherent talent, arresting but frustrated.

The most precocious, playful, puzzling and (with the
exception of Heaney) currently the most influential of all these
Northern Irish poets is Paul Muldoon. Since his first book,
New Weather, published in 1973 when he was only twenty-one,
Muldoon has teased the reader with droll anecdotes, innocent bits
of storytelling with a cool sense of leaving out the bits which
might 'make sense' of what he chooses to tell. Sometimes the
cryptic, reduced to a few lines, can at the same time be transparent,
as in the marvellously charged and menacing 'Ireland'*:

The Volkswagen parked in the gap,
But gently ticking over.
You wonder if it's lovers
And not men hurrying back
Across two fields and a river.

Muldoon's authority has increased with succeeding books,
particularly in the poem that dominates *Why Brownlee Left*

(1980), 'Immram'. This is a serio-comic mini-epic, in which the poet discovers his legendary ancestor Mael Duin, in terms of a strange mixture of tough Americanese and deliberately outrageous Irish blarney. These long ludic poems ('The More a Man Has the More a Man Wants', '7 Middagh Street', 'Madoc', most recently 'Yarrow' in *The Annals of Chile*, 1994) have become a feature of Muldoon's work: they are rambling, whimsical, making a peculiar virtue of apparent inconsequentiality.

It is these teasing, oblique and (to me) sometimes irritatingly bewildering semi-narratives that have especially entranced and influenced several of Muldoon's contemporaries and younger writers, some of them fellow-Irishmen, sometimes poets who share at least an Irish ancestry (such as Ian Duhig, whose work I shall look at in a later section), and some English poets who are seduced by what one critic, Neil Corcoran, has approvingly called Muldoon's 'slippery air of giving nothing away, at once cajoling and unaccommodating'.

I can partly understand this seductiveness, but actually am more convinced by many of Muldoon's shorter poems, early and late, such as 'The Right Arm', which effectively shows many of his gifts in miniature:

I was three-ish
when I plunged my arm into the sweet-jar
for the last bit of clove-rock.

We kept a shop in Eglish
that sold bread, milk, butter, cheese,
bacon and eggs,
Andrews Liver Salts,
and, until now, clove-rock.

I would give my right arm to have known then
how Eglish was itself wedged between
ecclesia and *église*.

The Eglish sky was its own stained glass vault
and my right arm was sleeved in glass
that has yet to shatter.

('The Right Arm')★

All these poets are from Northern Ireland. But whatever the
political boundaries are, there has for many years been a
strong sense of common ground and colleagiality between
poets North and South. Ancestrally, Yeats, Patrick Kavanagh,
MacNeice, Austin Clarke, John Hewitt, have all helped to
create a community of mixed idioms and concerns in Ireland.
In the South during the 1950s and 1960s Thomas Kinsella and
Richard Murphy in their different ways continued a devotion
to 'the well-made verse' which linked them with their younger
contemporaries in the North, such as Heaney, Longley and
Mahon.

The most surprising and idiosyncratic poet to emerge from
the South in recent years has now won a loyal audience not
only throughout Ireland but in England too. Paul Durcan is
emphatically *not* a devotee of 'the well-made verse'. Though
coming from a background in Dublin which in English terms
would be seen as conventional, even patrician (his father was a
judge), and a university degree from Cork in archaeology and
medieval history, Durcan in his emergent years might be seen
both as a rebel and a drop-out, doing odd jobs in London and
publishing with obscure Dublin presses. By 1982, when he was
thirty-eight, he had enough of an enthusiastic readership in the
North as well as the South to be given the accolade of a *Selected
Paul Durcan* in Belfast, edited by Michael Longley's powerful
and opinionated critic wife Edna.

It is easy to call many of Durcan's poems 'surrealist',
but that label much too narrowly restricts them to a kind
of academic literary history. Brendan Kennelly, the Dublin
poet and critic, has acutely commented on Durcan's 'manic
confidentiality, his blithe expositions of the seemingly
unthinkable, his hypnotic repetitions of what other poets would
hardly dare to utter once'. The terrible burdens of relationships
– parents, partners, pathos and pathology – in Durcan's poems

take off into regions which are totally unpredictable. Above all, his poems are very often disconcertingly funny, from their titles ('Hopping Round Knock Shrine in the Falling Rain, 1958', or 'The Only Man Never to Meet Samuel Beckett') right through to their triumphant unexpected conclusions.

Looking at his *A Snail in My Prime: New and Selected Poems* (significantly – and very successfully – published by a *London* publisher in 1993), I find it impossible effectively to quote Durcan in odd lines: his effects are cumulative, the products of letting an experience, or a wild surmise, take a walk inside his head. Anecdotal, discursive, stumbling and singing through freakish circumstances and imaginings, his poems tend to start from actual places (often in Ireland) and people one takes to be real (often members of his family). Numbing pain and helpless laughter joltingly alternate: sometimes one can't tell the difference.

To all this, Durcan adds something else – something which (like my lack of quotation from his work) one has to take on trust. His readings, which have now taken him to many parts of the world, throughout Europe and America, are spellbinding. And yet 'readings' is hardly the word: he recites, intones, soliloquises, entirely from memory – an exercise other poets have followed with considerably less success, especially in those cases where a seductive performance has been followed by one's reading of the actual text – diminishing, bewilderingly reduced, a stage-act shrunk down to nothing but disappointment. This is not so with Durcan: the rapt aural performance is reborn, revivified, on the page; and can be authenticated even by those who have never heard Durcan read.

13

'Pop' and after

In the 1985 version of this survey, I said that I found myself
taking an historical view of that phenomenon of the 1960s
and early 1970s, so-called 'pop' poetry. Even earlier, in
the first (1973) version, I described Christopher Logue and
Adrian Mitchell as 'two immediate forebears' of the pop poets.
Now, in 1995, these manoeuverings strike me as having the
quaint attitudes often struck by bewildered onlookers at an
archaeological dig, trying to make sense of something that
happened long, long ago.

During the past ten years, Logue has much more been
seen as the deviser and performer of his dramatic work
War Music, based on Homer, than as the biting Brechtian
and political satirist; and *War Music* has been successfully
added to in *Kings* and *The Husbands*. Mitchell has been
productive, and still entertains audiences with his funny and
warm-hearted hilarities and humanities; but it is the mixture
much as before. The original Liverpool poets, Adrian Henri,
Roger McGough and Brian Patten, also continue on the circuit,
and the professionalism and polish of their performances have
improved, so that now their familiarity is a genial business,
middle-aged audiences being reminded of the good old days,
younger ones learning to laugh along with their elders.

Their successors, some of whom I listed in 1985 (John
Cooper Clark, Linton Kwesi Johnson, 'Attila the Stockbroker'),
have been augmented by Benjamin Zephaniah and a whole
retinue of circuit performers, from the angry to the anodyne.
One of the most popular is John Hegley, who began his highly
successful cabaret career at the notoriously tough Comedy Store
in London in 1980 – a place in which the unfavoured are booed
off the stage within a few seconds. Hegley's success (not only
in front of very large audiences, including the Festival Hall,
but regularly in the pages of *The Guardian*) has been sneered
at and deplored by some critics, not all of them literary ones;
yet there is no doubt that his appearances, in these places, on

radio and television, have established him as an endearing oaf, whose lack of technique is itself a technique. Glasses, dogs, and difficulties about God have been his staple subjects. So has been his surprising rise from underdog, as in his well-known poem in which the title is longer than its complete couplet – 'A Poem About The Town of My Upbringing And The Conflict Between My Working-Class Origins And The Middle-Class Status Conferred Upon Me By My University Education':*

> I remember Luton
> As I'm swallowing my crout'n.

Hegley, and all the others I have mentioned, find themselves in the 1990s as fellow performers in a poetry scene very different from the 'sacramental jubilee' of the 1965 Albert Hall reading. Now, poets of very different persuasions from the populist pioneers (Logue, Mitchell, Henri, McGough, Patten) can find themselves in front of audiences which are at least as large, drawn there perhaps by something more demanding. Ted Hughes, Seamus Heaney, Tony Harrison, James Fenton, Wendy Cope, all have rapt and enthusiastic listeners whenever they appear. Such early promoters of the 'pop' scene as Michael Horovitz (one of the organisers of the 1965 Albert Hall event) still rant on about poetry's divisions; and I probably helped to fuel these antiquated rages with a broadcast talk I made in 1972, 'The Two Poetries', when it seemed to me that poetry was in danger of splitting up into a 'pop' camp and an academic one. Such fears now look out of date. The Festival Hall can be packed for Hughes on Monday, Harrison on Wednesday, and Hegley on Saturday. And the word 'pop' itself has a faded air, a stale smell: I shall be happy to abandon it.

14

Tony Harrison, Douglas Dunn, James Fenton, Wendy Cope

These comments on 'pop' poetry, and on audiences for poetry, lead me on to say something about a number of poets (some first emerging in the 1970s, others more recently) who have for very different reasons established themselves by now as popular, at least in the sense that their books sell many more copies than most so-called 'literary' novels in Britain today. Tony Harrison, Douglas Dunn, James Fenton and Wendy Cope have never attempted to ingratiate themselves; but each has found a devoted audience.

Both Tony Harrison and Douglas Dunn came from working-class backgrounds (Harrison in Leeds, Dunn in Scotland); they have continued to live their adult lives away from London (Harrison increasingly dividing his time between Newcastle and the United States, Dunn living first in Hull and then returning to Scotland more recently); and these facts have had a strong bearing on their poetry.

Tony Harrison's first full-length book, *The Loiners* (1970), is full of highly wrought poems, dense, strenuous, laced with proper names. He has worked in Nigeria and has travelled widely elsewhere, and there are comic as well as pungent exoticisms in his apostrophe to 'The White Queen':

Professor! Poet! Provincial! Dadaist!
Pathic, pathetic, half-blind and half-pissed
Most of these tours in Africa. A Corydon
Past fifty, fat, these suave looks gone,
That sallow cheek, that young Novello sheen
Gone matt and puffed. A radiant white queen
In sub-Saharan scrub I hold my court
On expat pay, my courtiers all bought.

Tony Harrison
Moira Conway

One of the longest poems in *The Loiners*, 'Newcastle is Peru',
takes its title from the seventeenth-century poet John Cleveland,
and there is something of Cleveland's manner in Harrison's
congested, fantastic, occasionally over-ingenious dazzling
flights. Harrison's poems are constantly aware of ironies and
oppositions, not least in his wry, sometimes bitter recognition of
his own cleverness and eloquence set against a traditionally dour
and reticent working-class Yorkshire upbringing:

> How you became a poet's a mystery!
> Wherever did you get your talent from?
>
> *I say*, I had two uncles, Joe and Harry –
> one was a stammerer, the other dumb.

('Heredity')★

This is the prefatory poem to *The School of Eloquence* (1978).
The poems in the title sequence, further expanded and added
to in *Continuous* (1981), are Harrison's central achievement
in coming to terms with society, class and language. They
are written in compactly rhyming sixteen-line 'sonnets', and
are by turns contemptuous, nostalgic, acid, affectionate: they
juxtapose Yorkshire dialect and Yorkshire speech with semantic
and lexicographical learning, and show the same pertinacious
and entertaining brilliance Harrison has brought to his widely
performed translations of Molière, Racine and Aeschylus. Other
poems in these books look more directly and personally, and
more movingly, at family lives and family deaths, as in the
poem on his mother's cremation:

Gold survives the fire that's hot enough
to make you ashes in a standard urn.
An envelope of coarse official buff
contains your wedding ring which wouldn't burn.

Dad told me I'd to tell them at St. James's
that the ring should go in the incinerator.
That 'eternity' inscribed with both their names is
his surety that they'd be together 'later'.

I signed for the parcelled clothing as the son,
this cardy, apron, pants, bra, dress –

the clerk phoned down: *6–8–8–3–1*?
Has she still her ring on? (slight pause) *Yes!*
It's on my warm palm now, your burnished ring!

I feel your ashes, head, arms, breasts, womb, legs,
sift through its circle slowly, like that thing
you used to let me watch to time the eggs.

('Timer')★

More recently, Harrison has augmented both his narrative and his polemical strengths, in such longer poems as 'A Kumquat for John Keats', 'The Red Lights of Plenty', 'The Lords of Life', 'Cypress & Cedar', and most influentially in a number of poems which have had a strong impact when seen and heard on television: *V* was the first of them, written during the 1984–85 miners' strike, and taking as its setting the vandalised graveyards in Leeds where his parents are buried. *A Cold Coming* appeared during the 1991 Gulf War, and extended his ambition to be a serious and controversial public poet. Though all these poems are written in Harrison's tightly controlled rhymed and metrical measures, they continue to confront and mingle such formalities with colloquial language, the cut and thrust of speech, and sometimes the rough richness of obscenities, in which the English language is peculiarly profuse and (as far as native speakers and listeners are concerned) peculiarly apt to be shocked and censorious: *V* in particular, on its first televised broadcast in 1987, caused a noisy debate between those who thought they heard nothing but gratuitous filth and those who recognised (and applauded) an audaciously assured assault on what has been characterised as one of the current English diseases, or at least disablements: 'gentility'.

In all this, I have no doubt that Harrison is both marvellously gifted and deeply serious: even for an Englishman who, through age, upbringing and idle inclination, might be thought to suffer from gentility, I am able to recognise what he has done. But – an odd irony for Harrison, who has given so much of his talent to translation (Middle English, French, Greek) – I have to say that I have a lurking notion that both his earlier concentration on English class-war in the English language and his more recent use of expletives and obscenities of the English sort have limited the universality he perhaps looks for. Australian and American readers – quite apart from non-native readers – are sometimes bewildered, not catching his 'register'. Poetry, famously, is the thing that cannot be translated; but some of the problems of Harrison's language are not exactly to do with translation.

Douglas Dunn's *Terry Street* (1969) took as its base a poor working-class part of Hull, a city which has appeared in some of Philip Larkin's poems too; but Dunn's are quite different in spirit and construction, lacking the finished and final quality of Larkin.

Douglas Dunn
Fay Godwin

Instead, they have a guarded quirkiness, an obliqueness, a hesitant cadence all his own, as in 'A Removal from Terry Street'★:

On a squeaking cart, they push the usual stuff,
A mattress, bed ends, cups, carpets, chairs,
Four paperback westerns. Two whistling youths
In surplus US Army battle-jackets
Remove their sister's goods. Her husband
Follows, carrying on his shoulders the son
Whose mischief we are glad to see removed,
And pushing, of all things, a lawnmower.
There is no grass in Terry Street. The worms
Come up cracks in concrete yards in moonlight.
That man, I wish him well, I wish him grass.

There may seem an artlessness about this observation, but it is deceptive in its slow, circumstantial rumination. Elsewhere in the book Dunn produced some bravura performances, such as the grotesque 'A Poem in Praise of the British'; and he went on in his next two books, *The Happier Life* (1972) and *Love or Nothing* (1974), to a wider variety of more complex things, not always with total conviction. It was with *Barbarians* (1979) that Dunn began to explore imaginatively something more congenial: he attempted to rediscover and repossess his own native country, Scotland, in terms both of class and of nationhood. This reached its finest form, technically and in feeling, in *St Kilda's Parliament* (1981), until then his best book. Among the considerable variety of this book, one of the most directly moving poems is the most personal, 'Washing the Coins', a childhood memory of lifting potatoes, among casual workers who were mostly Irish, of being mistaken for an Irish boy, and of being apologised to for the mistake:

> She knew me, but she couldn't tell my face
> From an Irish boy's, and she apologised
> And roughed my hair as into my cupped hands
> She poured a dozen pennies of the realm
> And placed two florins there, then cupped her hands
> Around my hands, like praying together.
> It is not good to feel you have no future.
> My clotted hands turned coins into muddy copper.
> I tumbled all my coins upon our table.
> My mother ran a basin of hot water.
> We bathed my wages and we scrubbed them clean.
> Once all that sediment was washed away,
> That residue of field caked on my money,
> I filled the basin to its brim with cold;
> And when the water had settled I could see
> Two English kings among their drowned Britannias.

> ('Washing the Coins')

Against the nostalgias and elegiac lamentations that perhaps dominate *St Kilda's Parliament* should be weighed much good humour about, and straightforward pleasure in, the things of this world, and a spacious range of other feelings – wry, indignant, ribald, sly, affectionate.

All these books helped to establish Dunn as a respected poet. But his breakthrough to a much wider audience came with what he managed to retrieve and commemorate of a tragic moment in middle life: the death from cancer of his first wife in the very year he published *St Kilda's Parliament*. His grief and the way in which he annotated, and in courageously exact terms followed, the progress of that grief found exemplary ground in *Elegies* (1985). This book clearly and poignantly spoke to many people, in its story-like pattern from patient anecdotal recital, through brief cameo portraits of his wife's brave composure, to the numbness and automaton-like aftermath of her death, and the slow recovery of something to cling to and hope for:

> They called me in. What moment worse
> Than that young doctor trying to explain?
> 'It's large and growing.' 'What is?' 'Malignancy.'
> 'Why *there*? She's an artist!'
>
> He shrugged and said 'Nobody knows.'
> He warned me it might spread. 'Spread?'
> My body ached to suffer like her twin
> And touch the cure with lips and healing sesames.
>
> No image, no straw to support me – nothing
> To hear or see. No leaves rustling in sunlight.
> Only the mind sliding against events
> And the antiseptic whiff of destiny.
>
> ('Second Opinion')
>
> To climb these stairs again, bearing a tray,
> Might be to find you pillowed with your books,

Your inventories listing gowns and frocks
As if preparing for a holiday.

                    ('The Kaleidoscope')

I think, and feel, and do, but do not know
All that I am, all that I have been, once,
Or what I could be could I think of it.

                    ('The Clear Day')

She spoke of what I might do 'afterwards'.
'Go, somewhere else.' I went north to Dundee.
Tomorrow I won't live here anymore,
Nor leave alone. *My love, say you'll come with me.*

                    ('Leaving Dundee')

Dunn has certainly not stood still since those memorable and
authoritative *Elegies. Northlight* (1988) and *Dante's Drum-kit*
(1993), particularly the latter, extended his range, not least
in showing his zestful humour, evident as early as 'Poem
in Praise of the British' in *Terry Street* almost a quarter of a
century earlier but now leaping into pawky life, as in such
poems as 'Extra Helpings', which plays unashamed tricks with
Edward Lear:

In our primary school
Set lunch was the rule
Though in Scotland we called that meal 'dinner'.
We tucked in like starvelings,
Inchinnan's wee darlings,
And it didn't make thin children thinner.

But what I liked best
Was disliked by the rest,
Rice pudding with raisins, and bloated sultanas,
Stewed fruit and dumplings
In big extra helpings
And hooray for first post-War bananas!

> *It was very good scoff*
> *So I polished it off*
> *A very dab hand with a spoon,*
> *a spoon,*
> *A very dab hand with my spoon.*

('Extra Helpings')

There is a jauntiness about several of Dunn's later excursions
(for example in 'Academy's Runners', 'Turn Over a New Leaf'
and 'Audenesques for 1960') which shows him enjoying himself
with the lighter side of seriousness. He seems to be at the height
of his powers.

James Fenton emerged in his very early twenties as an
heir of the games-playing (that is to say, later) Auden, but in
no obvious sense. In his first book, *Terminal Moraine* (1972),
he even reached back to an earlier Auden, that of 'Letter to
Lord Byron', in his brilliant Byronic-Audenesque political
and literary satire, 'Open Letter to Richard Crossman'. But
that book also contained bits of riddling rococo (such as 'The
Kingfisher's Boxing Gloves'), 'Our Western Furniture' (a long
and formal sequence of poems about the opening-up of Japan to
the West in the nineteenth century), and much else, including
'The Pitt-Rivers Museum, Oxford', which looks at this 'vast
gymnasium or barracks' and finds in its clutter of dusty, bizarre
and frightening objects a warning:

Go
As a historian of ideas or a sex-offender,
For the primitive art,

James Fenton

As a dusty semiologist, equipped to unravel
The seven components of that witch's curse
Or the syntax of the mutilated teeth. Go
In groups to giggle at curious finds.
But do not step into the kingdom of your promises
To yourself, like a child entering the forbidden
Woods of his lonely playtime.

After that book's publication, Fenton's activities as a political
journalist and as a foreign correspondent (in South-East Asia and
Germany) seemed for some years to distract him from poetry. A
few poems appeared in periodicals or in small pamphlets, but it
was not until his *The Memory of War* (1982), a collected volume
that took in much of *Terminal Moraine* and many later poems,
that it could be seen how his varied experiences, at home and

abroad, had borne fruit. 'A German Requiem' has a proverbial plainness, confronting guilt and the aftermath of war:

> His wife nods, and a secret smile,
> Like a breeze with enough strength to carry one dry leaf
> Over two pavingstones, passes from chair to chair.
> Even the enquirer is charmed.
> He forgets to pursue the point.
> It is not what he wants to know.
> It is what he wants not to know.
> It is not what they say.
> It is what they do not say.

A year later, that book was augmented, bringing in 'Children in Exile', a long poem which drew on his South-East Asian experience, and such troubling lyrics as 'Wind':*

> This is the wind, the wind in a field of corn.
> Great crowds are fleeing from a major disaster
> Down the long valleys, the green swaying wadis,
> Down through the beautiful catastrophe of wind.
>
> Families, tribes, nations and their livestock
> Have heard something, seen something. An expectation
> Or a gigantic misunderstanding has swept over the hilltop
> Bending the ear of the hedgerow with stories of fire and
> sword.
>
> I saw a thousand years pass in two seconds,
> Land was lost, languages rose and divided.
> This lord went east and found safety.
> His brother sought Africa and a dish of aloes.
>
> Centuries, minutes later, one might ask
> How the hilt of a sword wandered so far from the smithy.

And somewhere they will sing: 'Like chaff we were borne
In the wind'. This is the wind in a field of corn.

In Fenton's writing life, long periods of silence have been
punctuated with bursts of activity. Settling for a time in the
Phillipines, in 1989 he produced at his own expense *Manila
Envelope*, a large-format collection of new poems together with
something called 'The Manila Manifesto' and a poster. All this
seems to have been a way of testing the climate, of trying out a
new voice, or a range of voices. 'Voice' is an important concept
with Fenton: in his gnomic programme 'The Manila Manifesto',
he wrote:

What you need for poetry is a body and a voice. It doesn't
have to be a great body or a great voice. But it ought
ideally to be *your* body, and it ought to be *your* voice.

I feel that Fenton, with each impulse towards a new poem,
has to make it new. He listens attentively to the voices in his
head and, when the moment comes, it comes. And the whole
dazzling performance works because the craft, the techniques,
have been tuned and turned and made ready. Wherever one
turns in *Manila Envelope* (all of which went into a larger volume,
Out of Danger, published in an ordinary edition in 1993), there is
a feeling of rhythmical energy:

It started with a stabbing at a well
Below the minarets of Isfahan.
The widow took her son to see them kill
The officer who'd murdered her old man.
The child looked up and saw the hangman's work –
The man who'd killed his father swinging high.
The mother said 'My child, now be at peace.
The wolf has had the fruits of all his crime.'

From felony to felony to crime
From robbery to robbery to loss
From calumny to calumny to spite
From rivalry to rivalry to zeal

('The Ballad of the Imam and the Shah')

Tiananmen
Is broad and clean
And you can't tell
Where the dead have been
And you can't tell
What happened then
And you can't speak
Of Tiananmen.

('Tiananmen')

A shrieking man stood in the square
And he harangued the smart café
In which a bowlered codger sat
A-twirling of a fine moustache
A-drinking of a fine Tokay

And it was Monday and the town
Was working in a kind of peace
Excepting where the shrieking man
A-waving of his tattered limbs
Glared at the codger's trouser-crease

Saying

Coffee's mad
And tea is mad

And so are gums and teeth and lips
The horror ships that ply the seas
The horror tongues that plough the teeth
The coat
The tie
The trouser clips
The purple sergeant with the bugger-grips
Will string you up with all their art
And laugh their socks off as you blow apart.

('Ballad of the Shrieking Man')

Without courting popularity, these are popular poems; without taking notice of political debate, they are political; and they are often very grim and very funny at the same time. Fenton has now settled in England, and one wonders where the next impulse will come from, and how long one will have to wait.

Wendy Cope took longer to find her own voice and, paradoxically, when she did it was as a parodist. Her invention of Jason Strugnell, South London poet, man of letters, drinker and lecher, was one of the delights of the early 1980s, first broadcast on Radio 3, and then gathered together in her first full-length book, *Making Cocoa for Kingsley Amis*:

It was a dream I had last week
And some kind of record seemed vital.
I knew it wouldn't be much of a poem
But I love the title.

('Making Cocoa for Kingsley Amis')★

Cope's parodies (of Larkin, Heaney, Craig Raine, Geoffrey Hill, Peter Porter, Adrian Henri, and others) are brilliantly observed and cunningly written. But she is also a subversive and sly commentator on sex (especially on the many and various male

Wendy Cope
Mark Chichester-Clark

sexual hypocrisies) and on conventional causes and pomposities:
a statement by Ted Hughes ('The progress of any writer is
marked by those moments when he manages to outwit his
own inner police system') launches her into an extravaganza,
'A Policeman's Lot', based on W.S. Gilbert, and the fashion for
haiku prompts wonderfully deliberate banality:

> The cherry blossom
> In my neighbour's garden – oh!
> It looks really nice.

> ('Strugnell's Haiku':i)★

Cope's second book, *Serious Concerns*, extended this sort of
thing to underminings of the fashion for Green (environmental)

issues, psychiatrists, publishers, and (in 'Strugnell Lunaire')
the dreadfulness of lyrics-for-serious-music. The book also
continued its demolition of 'Bloody Men', 'Men and Their
Boring Arguments' and 'Tumps' (Typically Useless Male Poets),
but, as before, allowed some wan light to fall on love affairs,
their beginnings, middles and ends:

> When you're a spinster of forty,
> You're reduced to considering bids
> From husbands inclined to be naughty
> And divorcés obsessed with their kids.
>
> So perhaps you should wed in a hurry,
> But that has its drawbacks as well.
> The answer? There's no need to worry –
> Whatever you do, life is hell.

('Advice to a Young Woman')*

The wit, skill and sheer entertainment of such pieces made
Cope's two books best-sellers in the 1980s and 1990s, in spite
of some haughty or patronising dismissals of such 'light verse'.
She has avoided being enlisted into the feminist movement,
or being in any way bracketed off, as in her brisk couplet
which reacts against a remark in a review of her work ('They –
Roger McGough and Brian Patten – have something in common
with her, in that they write to amuse'):

> Write to amuse? What an appalling suggestion!
> I write to make people anxious and miserable and to worsen
>   their indigestion.

('Serious Concerns')*

If anyone in recent years has inherited the mantle of Stevie
Smith (an otherwise unrenewable garment) it is Wendy Cope.

15

Vernon Scannell, U.A. Fanthorpe, P.J. Kavanagh, Alistair Elliot, Andrew Motion, Blake Morrison, Sean O'Brien, Peter Reading

One of the commonest academic/aesthetic labels for many years has been 'post-modernist'. It tends to mean whatever its users want it to mean. Towards the end of the Introduction to their *Penguin Book of Contemporary Poetry* (1982), Blake Morrison and Andrew Motion said 'the poets included here do represent a departure, one which may be said to exhibit something of the spirit of post-modernism'. Since this anthology embraced twenty poets, from Seamus Heaney to Medbh McGuckian, from Tony Harrison to James Fenton, and from Douglas Dunn to Penelope Shuttle, that 'something' must be so capacious as to be practically meaningless.

Poets of earlier generations are apt to be wary of the term, and indeed to be robustly contemptuous of any literary discourse that smells of the academy. In some prefatory remarks, for example, to his *Collected Poems 1950–1993*, Vernon Scannell – now a veteran in his seventies – comments: ·

> At a time when much contemporary poetry seems to be written for specialist exegesists in the universities in order that they may practise their skills in 'deconstruction', I have, as Wordsworth said, 'wished to keep the reader in the company of flesh and blood, persuaded that by doing so I shall interest him'.

After a brief false start in the late 1940s, Scannell has held to his humane, colloquial, honest, demotic, elegiac, accurate, humorous, often eloquent and always well-made poems, ever since he first began to be noticed during the 1950s. At the time, he might easily have been fitted into the 'Movement' (his affinities are much more inclined towards Larkin, for example, than anyone else), and yet his doggedly professional path has avoided either recruitment into a school of poets or into the embrace of the academic canon. He has simply gone on writing poems with a persistent sense of questioningly telling the truth, as of 'The Long and Lovely Summers':

And yet we still remember them – the long
And lovely summers, never smeared or chilled –
Like poems, by heart; like poems, never wrong;
The idyll is intact, its truth distilled
From maculate fact, preserved as by the sharp
And merciful mendacities of art.

There are other poets, more or less of Scannell's generation (Patricia Beer, Laurence Lerner) and rather younger (U.A. Fanthorpe, P.J. Kavanagh, Alistair Elliot), of whom the same is true. Patricia Beer is more quizzical, Laurence Lerner more restlessly inventive, but what they share is a sense of a poem as being a well-made object, and something made by a truth-teller, won from experience, rather than an artful artefact which has more to do with games-playing than seeing things as they are.

   U.A. Fanthorpe is a self-confessed drop-out, someone who made a decision to leave her demanding job as a senior English teacher at one of the best-known independent girls' schools and work as a hospital clerk. The sense of release this gave her allowed her to begin writing the poems which, when she was almost fifty, were gathered together and published in her first book, *Side Effects* (1978). The title-poem (or rather the poem which obliquely refers to it, 'Not My Best Side') is a marvellously funny triptych based on Uccello's painting 'St George and the Dragon', in which dragon, maiden and saint in turn speak their feelings. But most of these earlier Fanthorpe poems are based, clearly and circumstantially, on her daily life at work, such as 'From the Remand Centre'*:

Eleven stone and nineteen years of want
Flex inside Koreen. Voices speak to her
In dreams of love. She needs it like a fag,
Ever since Mum, who didn't think her daft,
Died suddenly in front of her. She holds
Her warder lovingly with powerful palms,
Slings head upon her shoulders, cries *Get lost*,
Meaning *I love you*, and her blows caress.

Later poems spread out to embrace all kinds of subject
matter – voices out of history, literature, the foothills of
education, and ordinary experience, done with wit and feeling.
U.A. Fanthorpe has cut through to many readers who have
avoided contemporary poetry until coming across her work,
with its refreshing sense of real people, real worlds.

   Faithfulness to the real is part of the force behind
P.J. Kavanagh's poems too. He is wryly aware of this in the
concluding lines of 'Doggerel':

Today I thought it time to write this down,
Beyond decoration, humble, in plain rhyme,
As clear as I could, and as truthful, which I have done.

Kavanagh has several times paid homage to Edward Thomas
and Louis MacNeice: he is faithful to their example in the way
he writes of natural things, in his discursiveness, and in his
willingness to let himself be guided by tentative rhythms:

This snow, thaw, frost, thaw and rain
Has bitten great gaps in the old limestone
Walls that summer visitors delighted in:
Dark grey, with rusty orange and sky-grey lichen
And mosses green as cress; they caught the sun
Pink in the morning and, white under the moon,
Shadowed the fox. They have fallen down,

Nor will be, nor should be, built again,
Fences being cheaper; they are done
That were my passion. Foxes' navigation, weasels' run,
Skilful catchers of every light, they open
Like graves, a jumble of yellow bone
That tractors tidy away. Visitors from the town
May vaguely remark an absence, travel on.

The thud, thud, is fence-posts going in.

                              ('News from Gloucestershire')*

From the same generation, Alistair Elliot is a poet whose
more recent poems have at last brought him some of the
recognition due him for many years. He first made an impact
as an undergraduate in the early 1950s, when in the Oxford
of the time he was as much admired as Geoffrey Hill by
his contemporaries. But a long, rather unproductive period
followed. Then, in the late 1970s, there began a succession of
books, including the ingenious conversation pieces in *Talking
Back* (1982) and the discursive narrative poem *On the Appian
Way* (1984), entertainingly following the route of Horace, the
Roman poet.

What one finds in Elliot's poems is a curious mind
searching experience, learnedly, lightly, and coming back
with strange tales to tell and ruminations to offer: part of his
childhood spent in wartime America (and return journeys), a
period living in Iran, family and ancestral lore from Scotland
– all these are mixed in with perceptions of the oddities of
everyday life, as in 'An Old Theory of Vision'*, which comes
from Elliot's most recent book, *Turning the Stones* (1993):

How do I see you? You are over there
casually scratching your unimprovable neck
with your left hand; your image comes through the air
inexhaustibly, as long as I can look,
and visible from the door, the floor, this chair.

Lucretius would have said you were casting off
a film of skin, one coat of molecules,
like a mayfly's exoskeleton, a snake's slough;
that what I see is an ecdysis of veils,
things stripping themselves of infinitesimal stuff.

'So thin they don't get in each other's way' –
too thin to kiss – these simulacra peel
and float away, all over. We might say
things would wear down to nothing; all that foil
would stifle us – unless it could decay.

'Most of it does – but sometimes some remains,
the old look of a person. That's a ghost.'
Oh comfortable theory, that explains
I may still see you when your body's lost –
longer, more often, and without such pains.

Meanwhile the photons come and go between us
without confusion, taking images
for rides, to where there may be retinas
or not, with minds to read the touching messages –
delivered upside-down and from a distance.

In the 1984 version of this survey, I said of Andrew Motion's
work that it was permeated with 'a melancholy ache of loss'.
This reaction was based chiefly on Motion's only full-length
book at that time, *The Pleasure Steamers* (1978), though I
mentioned the subsequent longish narrative-monologue
'Independence', which was separately published in 1981.

Since then, in a number of books, that 'melancholy ache
of loss' has made plain its origin, putting both his earlier and
later poems into perspective. The prose piece 'Skating' (included
in *Dangerous Play: Poems 1974–1984*) sets down precisely and
sensitively an account of how Motion's mother, after a riding
accident, lay comatose in hospital for ten years during his teens

and early adulthood, and then died. It would be glib to see this experience as wholly determining Motion's inclinations and strategies in his poetry, but it does seem to help account for his emotional wariness, and his muted understatements. Adopting another persona (as in 'The Letter', 'Independence' and 'Bathing at Glymenopoulo') was for a time a way of pushing away from personal experience, and also a way of telling stories.

Motion was a friend of Larkin's and after Larkin's death became his biographer. 'This is your subject speaking', his poem in memory of Larkin, is a beautifully judged re-creation of a person and a personality, weaving together observation, memory, snatches of speech, with affection and accuracy. Motion's last two books, *Love in a Life* (1991) and *The Price of Everything* (1994), have ventured more boldly and inventively into verse autobiography, using a greater variety of manners and styles – ballad-like, calling on refrains and repetitions, employing prose, and using rhyme rather more than formerly. The vicissitudes of marriages, children and memories of his own childhood, his father's war and (in 'Joe Soap') a strange conspectus or kaleidoscope of wars; these devices and themes, together with a wider range of attack, make Motion's recent poetry more interesting than his earlier work:

The border was neither wide nor deep, but it took a day
to sieve it, working through sprays of gravel, London clay,
and bonfire wrecks left by people before us:
sheets of sick iron, charred bottles, batteries leaking pus.

I thought of Joanna; the brittle white china body
I smashed, she smashed and hid, but which still cuts me
out of the deep solid earth wrestling and fretting like the sea.

('The Great Globe')★

Blake Morrison's progress, in his two books followed by his 1994 poem specially created for television on the James Bulger child-murder case, has been towards monologue and narrative.

135

Half his first book (*Dark Glasses*, 1984) was taken up with a long semi-dramatic poem on secrecy and deception, 'The Inquisitor', which took material from the death of the Italian banker Roberto Craxi, the life of Lech Walesa, and the Falklands war, and transmuted them:

> There are no ends, though, and no answers, for this
> Is secrecy, whose art is to withhold
> The logic it is richer not to know.
> The world at large behind the berberis
> Cannot be caught, not quite.

Much more daringly, in the title-poem of *The Ballad of the Yorkshire Ripper* (1987) Morrison took on the mask and artifice of Yorkshire dialect to delve into the psychology of the serial killer Peter Sutcliffe:

> Ower t'ills up northways
> stormclouds thump an drain
> like opened blood-black blisters
> leakin pus and pain.
>
> An death is like a stormclap,
> a frizzling o thi cells,
> a pitchfork through thi arteries
> and tha knows there in't owt else.
>
> It meks me think on Peter,
> an what e did an why,
> an ow mi mates ate women,
> and how Peter med em die.

Morrison is an excellent journalist as well as a poet, and part of the appeal of his work is its present-ness, its sense of having a keen nose for poetry-as-news.

This, combined with a strong and sometimes aggressive social sense, is shared by Sean O'Brien. There is an undercurrent of anger in many of O'Brien's poems, at its most ferociously and openly contemptuous in 'Song of the South', from his second book, *The Frighteners* (1987):

We change our cars and eat our meat.
There are no negroes on our street.
Our sons are sailing with the fleet.
We keep our mania discreet . . .

Conservative in politics,
We have no time for lefty pricks
Who sympathise with wogs and spicks.
We print the kind of shit that sticks

[. . .]

It is of property we dream.
We like to think we are a team.
We think that poverty's a scream.
We're still more vicious than we seem

There is also a ruefully funny scrutiny of such things as he loathes yet somehow loves, as in 'Hatred of Libraries' (with its concomitant 'Notes on the Use of the Library (Basement Annexe)', or 'In Residence: A Worst Case View', all of which come from *HMS Glasshouse* (1991). It is the sheer verve of O'Brien that keeps one reading, and the energy of his exasperation.

The prolific and inventive Peter Reading has produced a large number of books in the past twenty years, and almost from the start they have been unified sequences, which increasingly make cross-references to their own precursors. He weaves together narratives, bits of 'found' material (some of which he must have invented), different voices; and his later

Peter Reading

books actually take on the deliberate appearance of drafts, palimpsests, and damaged manuscripts.

All this is in the cause of a restlessly fiction-making urge, which at the same time is alert to reportage, particularly of the black, the grim, and the fantastic. *Fiction* (1979) was the first of Reading's books to draw specific attention to this urge, followed by others which explored madness, cruelty, cancer, the homeless, terrorism. There is, however, a case for saying that this is not the important thing about Reading: what he uniquely has is an obsessive craftsmanship, at ease with every kind of verse-form, matched with a macabre, bizarre sense of humour. He relishes the stately and the ceremonial, as much as he keeps his ears open for the demotic, the inarticulate, the speechless. Because of the composed unity of Reading's books, he is almost impossible to quote from. But there is one mock-sacerdotal section from *Ukulele Music* (1985) which gives at least a taste of his mordant tone:

This is unclean: to eat turbots on Tuesdays,
tying the turban unclockwise at cockcrow,
cutting the beard in a south-facing mirror,
wearing the mitre whilst sipping the Bovril,
chawing the pig and the hen and the ox-tail,
kissing of crosses with peckers erected,
pinching of bottoms (except in a yashmak),
flapping of cocks at the star-spangled banner,
snatching the claret-pot off of the vicar,
munching the wafer without genuflexion,
facing the East with the arse pointing backwards,
thinking of something a little bit risqué,
raising the cassock to show off the Y-fronts,
holding a Homburg without proper licence,
chewing the cud with another man's cattle,
groping the ladies – or gentry – o'Sundays,
leaving the tip on the old-plum-tree-shaker,
speaking in physics instead of the Claptrap,
failing to pay due obeisance to monkeys,
loving the platypus more than the True Duck,
death without Afterlife, smirking in Mecca,
laughing at funny hats, holding the tenet
how that the Word be but fucking baloney,
failing to laud the Accipiter which Our Lord saith is
Wisdom.

Started by *Australopithecus*, these are
time-honoured Creeds (and all unHoly doubters
shall be enlightened by Pious Devices:
mayhems of tinytots, low-flying hardwares,
kneecappings, letterbombs, deaths of the firstborns,
total extinctions of infidel unclean wrong-godded
others).

16

John Fuller, Hugo Williams, Craig Raine, Christopher Reid, Kit Wright, John Whitworth, Peter Scupham, John Mole, George Szirtes

Roy Fuller once said (in a broadcast after the death of John Betjeman) that, whatever demurs and embarrassments English people in general feel when they are faced with poetry, they can – and sometimes do – acknowledge sheer technical skill, in poems as in, say, football.

Fuller was thinking not only of Betjeman but of Robert Burns (whose reputation stretches well beyond convivial celebrations of his birthday in Scotland) and of Rudyard Kipling. Without actually mentioning them, and not mentioning them because they are hardly household names, he might have been thinking in our own time of his son, John Fuller; of James Fenton, whom Roy Fuller admired at an early stage; and of Clive James, now an international figure, but not because of his poetry.

Beyond this, the delight in the well-made poem – which is not necessarily to say the *conventionally* well-made poem – is apparent even in these contentious days. Certainly John Fuller, as teacher (in Oxford) and poet, has been an exemplary person, the mentor and encourager of many. His best-known pupil is James Fenton, but simply to list those aspirant poets who have been through his pedagogic hands would take up more space in this survey that I can afford.

John Fuller's own work has stretched from his precociously witty and sophisticated poems in his youth (his first book was published in 1961, when he was only twenty-three) to later ventures into much more complex and often riddling things, more ambitious and at greater length. His *Selected Poems*

1954–1982 is a good sample, stretching back to work written when he was still in his teens, such as 'Fairy Tale', a sonnet which challenges Auden on his own ground:

> But worse than all the sniggers of the wood,
> The waiting Prince was ugly, pale and good.

He has always been a wonderfully sprightly inventor of situations and stories, a spinner of complicated yarns. One of his most original pieces has been 'The Most Difficult Position', two linked monologues which follow a mid-nineteenth-century battle between opponents in chess; and his full-length verse-novel, *The Illusionists*, anticipated several later attempts to give the Victorian verse-novel a new setting.

Of course 'skill' is an elastic word: it doesn't necessarily imply rigid formality of a received sort. Ian Hamilton's brief pregnant lyrics, which for a time were so influential in the 1970s, are consummate performances without following any existing guidelines; and those who followed him have either fallen silent or have struck out in other directions – most notably Hugo Williams who, after a period of coming under Hamilton's minimalist spell, has established an entirely new reputation as the recorder of his upbringing as son of bohemian actor/playwright parents, in a discursive, anecdotal, quizzical series of poems which commemorate, comment on, subvert and wander away from a personal experience which Williams – skilfully – turns into universal experience.

Quite different from this was what Craig Raine and Christopher Reid were up to in their first books published in the late 1970s and early 1980s; yet they, too, were part of the John Fuller School of Skill. It was quickly noticed that here was something – not immediately recognised as an offshoot – which deserved to be granted its own name, that of the so-called 'Martians', taking the title from the title-poem of Raine's second book, *A Martian Sends a Postcard Home* (1979): in it, everyday objects are presented as bizarre discoveries, as if for the first time:

Caxtons are mechanical birds with many wings
and some are treasured for their markings –

they cause the eyes to melt
or the body to shriek without pain.

I have never seen one fly, but
sometimes they perch on the hand.

Christopher Reid followed the same pattern, though in his
case the measures in which he wrote were more playful, less
mechanically declarative, as in his image of pigs' heads on the
counter of a butcher's shop:

With ears like wings, these pallid putti –
hideous symbols of eternal beauty –

relax on parsley and smirk about
their newly-disembodied state.

('H. Vernon')

For a time the influence of this sort of thing was widespread,
to be noticed in many poets both younger and older. But it
was short-lived; and indeed both Raine and Reid went on to
other things, Reid adopting for example the invented persona
of a Central European woman (*Katerina Brac*), and then taking
off into much more fragmented struggles with language in *The
Echoey Tunnel* (1991), in which a woman's dire illness and an
old man's memories are, distinctly and separately, given their
own desperate voices. Raine much more ambitiously, and I
think with a mistaken wilfulness, produced a novel-length verse
narrative, *History: The Home Movie* (1994), which attempted to
link together two family histories, his wife's (she is one of the
Russian Pasternaks) and his own.

More readily acceptable skill has been seen over these years in Kit Wright and John Whitworth. In some ways Wright is a straightforwardly comic poet, and he has marked rhythmical energy. He has written much very funny verse for young children, and there is always a lightness of touch in what he does. But he is not simply an entertainer: there is grimmer stuff there, whether in his masterly 'Versions of Dr Tyerly' (on nineteenth-century ideas about how to treat lunatics) or in his more personal poems about mental stress, breakdown, the terrors of drink, or lost loves. Nevertheless, it is the dazzlingly funny precision of phrase and rhythm which one most remembers in his *Poems 1974–1983*, daring to take on, with obscene relish, the sanctities of BBC radio's long-lived soap opera 'The Archers' (in 'Underneath the Archers or What's all this about Walter's Willy?'), or jauntily retailing a blackly humorous anecdote ('Bump-Starting the Hearse').

Kit Wright has shown his admiration of Gavin Ewart's example quite openly, in his formal variety, his humour, and his refusal to make distinctions between 'good taste' and 'bad taste'. So, even more openly, has John Whitworth. (Philip Larkin commented that Whitworth was 'a worthy addition to the meanwhile-back-to-real-life school fathered by Gavin Ewart'). He has a cheeky, breezy, even sometimes hearty way with him, puncturing pretensions, cheerfully acknowledging the ribald, rueful views of *l'homme moyen sensuel*; and what chiefly marks him out is the range and dash of his verse forms, as various as Ewart's:

> Life is a beanbag stuffed with tintacks
> And you'll inflate it like a bladder.
> Deep-fry in influences, and a
> Ratatouille of fractured syntax,
> Lard with significance and season
> With simile and metaphor
> Unapt, inept as heretofore,
> A dash of rhyme, a smidge of reason,
> But not too much. Your synthesis
> Is rank and spiky, full of piss

And should do well among the cog-
noscenti on a Critics' Forum.
Readers? No danger. You won't bore 'em.
They lost you in a mental fog
About the time of Rupert Brooke
Or Flecker (Who reads Flecker now?
I do. Shut up.) and anyhow
No common person reads a book.
Your telly's done for all that guff. It
's hard and boring. You can stuff it.

('The Middle-sized Poem')

There is wit, too, but of a gentler kind, in some of Peter
Scupham's poems, such as the affectionate anecdotal poems in
memory of his father in *Watching the Perseids* (1990). Scupham's
scrupulous, measured language is much concerned with survivals
and continuities, with mortality and buried experience, and it
is organised with a lavish but extremely disciplined care, well
exemplified in his sonnet-sequence which gives the title to *The
Hinterland* (1977) – fifteen poems dexterously woven together into
a tapestry, the theme of which is the First World War. A poem
that catches in miniature something of the flavour of Scupham is
'This Evening', one of a short elegiac sequence for his mother:

I watch you turning into memory,
Becoming something far too sharp, and clear.
You dwindle on the bed, and make a space
As small as Alice, waiting far from here

In rooms the size of photographs, on sands
By seas whose waters could not brim a cup;
Dressed in an inch or two of brilliant light:
Profound, and serious, and un-grownup.

As if you spend this evening trying on
The proper size to slip into a head,
Knowing how small the clothes are that must fit
That plain and simple hugeness: being dead.

('This Evening')★

John Mole has been closely associated with Peter Scupham
in running the Mandeville Press, a small concern which has
been responsible for the fine and sensitive production of many
pamphlets of poems for several years. Mole's own work is
craftsmanly, clear, sharp, economical, with often a lightness of
touch and a confrontation with mystery:

Dear Doctor Universe,
Your medicine ball
Is our dream bolus,
A coveted cure-all:
These are the ropes
And we are learning them.

('Learning the Ropes')

Life is not a stroll across a field.
Whatever else it is it isn't that.
And luck is something more than the black cat
Which crossed your path just once when, still a child,
You thought there was no other beast in view –
That pussens sauntered by for none but you.

He didn't. Not a whisker left to chance
The necessary journey that he took
Out of his picture in your story book

To where your own son's wilful innocence
Finds and returns him, still beguiled
By life that seems a stroll across a field.

('On a Line from Pasternak')★

George Szirtes came to England as a small boy after the
1956 uprising in Hungary, and trained here first as a painter
and graphic artist. His early poems (in *The Slant Door*, 1979)
showed an acute visual perception in his shaping of a seen
world, juxtaposing details with both clarity and suggestions of
something beyond and behind, as in:

I say there will be hopelessness before
The children rise and the chair topples back:
The bright, transparent skins will fold and crack
Before the painter leaves by the back door.

('Group Portrait with Pets')

In 1984 Szirtes made a return journey to Hungary, which he had
not seen since he was a child. The first fruits of this rediscovery
of his native place can be found in *The Photographer in Winter*
(1986). Familiarity and strangeness mingle:

Think of a glove turned neatly inside out;
think of your hand running along a rail
as children run down galleries grown stale
with refuse; think of hands reversed; of keys
and locks; think of these blocks as hollow trees
still echoing to something inchoate;

think of fear, precise as a clean hand
searching in dark corners, with a skill
that years of practice manage to instil;

think of locks where keys will never turn;
of rooms where it takes experts to discern
a movement that the eye can't understand:

The inchoate is what gets lost. You hear
a crazy woman singing . . . *Tannenbaum,
O tannenbaum* . . . but then her words become
confused with curses, shouts of *God* and *Fate*,
and this is not exactly inchoate
but in such imprecision there is fear.

('The Courtyards: 2')*

This process of repossessing Hungary has continued in later
visits and later books. Szirtes was in Budapest during the great
changes of 1989, and in *Bridge Passages* (1991) he sees the events
obliquely, against the background of his childhood, his first
confrontation with England and the English language, and his
gradual mastery of an adult language of which he had lost all
but a child's knowledge – Hungarian: this is shown in several
fine translations of Otto Orban. And in 'Unter den Linden'*, he
demonstrates his ironical formal skills by deliberately choosing
to write in that unlikely and otherwise faded old-fashioned form,
the rondeau:

In Unter den Linden and Wenceslas Square
the candles wink their *laissez-faire*,
people are trampling over borders,
packing their luggage. Cassette recorders
hiss like steam in the cold air,

cameras roll and spokesmen prepare
brief noncommittal statements, tear
pages from notebooks and wait for orders.
Prisons open: prisoners and warders
　　mix in Unter den Linden.

In Prague and Budapest they wear
rosettes, wave flags. A furious year
gathers to a close. The wind disorders
ships of state, and fleets of boarders.
Men link hands, dance and boldly stare
　　across Unter den Linden.

17

Some women

Elsewhere in this survey, I discuss a number of women poets, from Stevie Smith to Wendy Cope and Carol Ann Duffy. To corral others of them together in this section is, I would agree, a convenient and even a lazy ploy, rather than an intelligent critical act. And yet to do this is, in a sense, to follow a common practice, inaugurated by women, since the 1970s: anthologies, even whole publishing houses, have presented women as women.

They are, of course, individuals, however they may be presented. It would be impossible, for example, to find much in common in three senior figures, now in their eighties: Kathleen Raine, E.J. Scovell and Anne Ridler have never through their long writing careers been associated in any way. Kathleen Raine has followed her own mystical path as someone who sees herself as in the line of Blake. E.J. Scovell had some notice in the 1950s, but it was not until *The Space Between* (1982) and her later *Collected Poems* that she was properly recognised as a writer of immaculate grace and penetrating poignancy. Anne Ridler, with a more metaphysical sharpness, has been even more pushed into the margins (after an early start in which she was encouraged by T.S. Eliot), and it is only very recently, with her own *Collected Poems*, that she has been rediscovered.

A later generation, or perhaps one should speak of two generations, has found its own unbroken distinction: Jenny Joseph, Fleur Adcock, Freda Downie (who died recently), and then Carol Rumens, Vicki Feaver, Carole Satyamurti – all of them have been noticed for their individuality. There was the disconcerting eruption of Fiona Pitt-Kethley, who after a plodding start began to write poems which – perhaps too programmatically – both delighted and shocked an audience (which I suspect was and is largely male) with flatly declarative stuff about the awful vanities of men and the unsatisfied lusts of women, sardonic reports from the sexual battlefront, calculated to make the reader at the same time snigger and fidget with

Carol Ann Duffy
Sue Adler

embarrassment. And the 'New Generation Poets', referred to elsewhere in this survey, included not only Carol Ann Duffy and Kathleen Jamie but Moniza Alvi, Elizabeth Garrett, Sarah Maguire, Lavinia Greenlaw, Pauline Stainer and Susan Wicks.

In all this, I can't find anything like the battle-lines that have been drawn up by the feminist movement in America – for example, the central figure there of Adrienne Rich, who, beginning as an exact and memorable formalist in the early 1950s, then broke away and has become the spokeswoman of defiant women: polemical, free, lesbian. Rich is an important writer – at least in the way that she has had an important effect on her fellow American women writers – but it would be hard to find an equivalent in Britain, without turning to writers who are not (or not primarily) poets: Germaine Greer, Jeanette Winterson.

But in Britain, what I think I *can* say is that the generations of women poets who were faced with, or who actually grew up with, the feminist revolutions of the post-1960s have not been able to ignore what has gone on; nor have they wished to. Fleur Adcock's elegant, colloquial, astringent, ironical poems (for example, 'Against Coupling') have very precisely caught a tone from the prevailing air – but this can look like a circular argument; did she catch the tone, or did she help to achieve it? Vicki Feaver's first book, *Close Relatives* (1981), contained many poems which were concerned with the tensions and pleasures of ordinary domestic life: husbands and wives, mothers and children, children in relation to their parents, in a very clear, tender, wistful way, often touched with pathos. But when, after a long gap, she produced her second book, *The Handless Maiden* (1994), the difference was marked. She had become stranger, fiercer, and also wittier ('Thinking of new ways to kill you/I might try drowning you in the lily pond'). These confrontations with childhood and with love gone sour are sly, stylish, quietly getting under one's skin. Vicki Feaver, along with Wendy Cope and Carol Ann Duffy, is to me the best of the post-1960 generation.

Women poets, or poets who are women (all these devices are clumsy), have a high profile in the late twentieth century. When they, or we, seek ancestors, there is a confusion. Elizabeth Barrett (who married Robert Browning) was in her lifetime a far more highly regarded poet than her husband, and was seriously considered for the post of Poet Laureate – and this in Victorian England, conventionally seen as a wholly male reserve. Emily Dickinson, her contemporary in America, had no success at all until she died – but almost immediately forces were mustered which soon established her as the greatest poet America has ever produced. In this survey, Stevie Smith, Elizabeth Jennings, U.A. Fanthorpe, Wendy Cope, Carol Ann Duffy, Liz Lochhead, Kathleen Jamie, and others, have been noticed and appraised with as much warmth and sense of judgement as I can muster. It is hard for a man to dispute this disputed ground. The bibliography at the end will, at least, I hope fend off indignant voices which may attempt to accuse me of 'marginalising' – or, indeed, blankly ignoring.

18

'The New Generation'

In 1994, *Poetry Review*, allying itself with the sort of promotional tactics which hitherto in the book world had seemed the province of such successful campaigns as that which has given the annual Booker Prize for fiction a high (if sometimes derided or deplored) profile, took part in 'The New Generation'. Twenty young, or youngish, poets were for a time given much attention in the press, on radio and television, and in readings up and down the country. Publishers and booksellers were rallied to the cause.

The most promoted poets were Simon Armitage, Carol Ann Duffy, and Glyn Maxwell; not far behind came Michael Donaghy, Ian Duhig, and Don Paterson. For a time, it almost seemed that poetry had turned into the World Cup, with the newspapers gossiping about how much money individual poets could command for readings, and other such marks of public favour.

Some have said that these tactics can do nothing but good for poets, and poetry, in general, and that the sales of books of poetry, not just by these promoted poets but by all poets, have benefited. My final chapter in this survey, on 'The Poetry Business', throws some cold water on such euphoria. And yet it would be wrong not to recognise that more good than harm has been done by all this excited talk. What is much more difficult is to pick out from the offered field of players those who seem to justify the campaign.

Simon Armitage was quickly noticed in the late 1980s: his first book, *Zoom*, published in 1989, drew both directly and quirkily on his everyday world (industrial Yorkshire and Lancashire, pub talk, slangy anecdotes from schooldays and from his daily work as a probation officer), with a confidence, even a brashness, that marked him out as someone to watch. 'Bus Talk', 'Poem by the Boy outside the Fire Station', 'Ten Pence Story', are all very much pieces for speaking, cheekily direct slices of life given energy by the sheer force of Armitage's attack, both rhetorical and laconic.

Simon Armitage
Jason Bell

Disappearance and evasiveness are as much part of Armitage's tactics as such buttonholing techniques; and in this a continuing obsession is Weldon Kees, the American poet who vanished, a probable suicide, in San Francisco in 1955. Armitage's second book, *Kid* (1992), contained several 'Robinson' poems, which took their persona from Kees' work. Tough, mysterious and playful all at once, these poems share something with Paul Muldoon's 'Immram'. They are puzzles, the appeal of which to some readers seems to be that they don't demand answers:

You'd wake to the simple sounds of housework.
How I rose from that makeshift double-bed,
dressed in silence, then stacked the fire
without so much as stirring you, was beyond you.

From the far corner, twisting a duster
through the silverware, I'd watch as your eyes
became accustomed to the light. You'd smile;
I'd move on to the next object.

Robinson, a friend of a friend of mine
tells me you've been talking in a tone of voice
I don't much care for. A word of warning:
that morning when I sharpened a pencil

and spelt it out in capital letters, I meant it.
And another thing, darling: as I ran
my gently trembling tongue along the gummed edge
of the envelope, I was smiling.

('Dear Robinson')*

Indeed, my chief problem in reading Armitage is that a lot of
the time I find it difficult – or impossible – to follow what he
is saying. I enjoy the sensation of someone being very bright,
streetwise, racy, someone who can mix West Yorkshire idiom
with more Parnassian language, and who knows how to turn
a line and spin a tale. But, particularly with *Book of Matches*
(1993), I find that, when I try to write a marginal paraphrase,
or a précis, the whole thing too often seems to collapse into
banalities, when what I think Armitage is after is ironies.

This seems so with, for example, one of the title-sequence
pieces, behind which one can hear the example of Auden's
currently revived 'Stop all the clocks . . .':

I thought I'd write my own obituary. Instead,
I wrote the blurb for when I'm risen from the dead:

Ignite the flares, connect the phones, wind all the clocks;
the sun goes rusty like a medal in its box –
collect it from the loft. Peg out the stars,
replace the bulbs of Jupiter and Mars.

A man like that takes something with him when he dies,
but he has wept the coins that rested on his eyes,
eased out the stopper from the mouthpiece of the cave,
exhumed his own white body from the grave.

Unlock the rivers, hoist the dawn and launch the sea.
Set up the skittles of the orchard and the wood again,
now everything is clear and straight and free and good again.

('I thought I'd write my own obituary . . .')*

'Armitage has been likened to Auden for his versatility,
confidence and originality' (*Poetry Review*); so has Glyn
Maxwell, whose metrical, rhythmical and syntactical trickery
is even more marked than Armitage's. Sometimes the jumpily
energetic urge to startle, entertain, amuse, can look like a
nervous and even ingratiating tic, and sometimes Maxwell's
longer poems outstay their welcome, as in the title-poem of his
first book, *Tale of the Mayor's Son* (1990), a masterly exercise
in pointlessness. His taste for elaboration and conjuring with
drama continued in *Out of the Rain* (1992), and was given full
licence in his collection of three verse plays, *Gnyss the Magnificent*
(1993): I have seen none of these performed (they have been
shown in Maxwell's back garden in Welwyn Garden City), but
on the page they are not very much more convincing than the
once-hailed verse drama of Stephen Phillips, which had a brief
notorious success in the early years of this century.

However, Maxwell at his best has a bright sense of style
which can be jokingly lyrical:

He was a great ambassador for the game.
                He had a simple name.
His name was known in households other than ours.
                But we knew other stars.
We could recall as many finalists
                as many panellists.
But when they said this was his Waterloo,
                we said it was ours too.

('Sport Story of a Winner')

And in 'Video Tale of a Patriot' his ingenuity is very
entertaining:

START. Eton. Hice. Beaten
in some grim urban/hopeless northern
seat. Afforded southern chances.
        Rosette. Recount. Speech. Dances.
Member. Lobbies. Froth. Committees.
        Old wife. New wife. Boards. City's.
Sir. Riches. Burgundy. Soak.
        Lord. Bypass. Bypass. Croak.

Sorry, REWIND: bypass-bypass-
        lord-soak-burgundy-riches-
sir. PLAY. 'Sir: I am increasingly
concerned at the let's say increasingly
unpredictable, unclassifiable,
        unconstructive, unreliable,
incomprehensible, reprehensible,
        a-moral, im-moral, not very sensible

acts of citizens of England of late.
        Acts not actually threatening the State
but thoroughly disconcerting. Sir:
        I saw a her who was kissing a her

It could be said that such high-spirited stuff picks extremely easy
targets, and indeed practically all Maxwell's originality seems to
be deployed on 'style'. I feel that if Armitage and Maxwell are
to be seen as heirs of Auden, they need a bit more solidity than
they have so far shown.
    Don Paterson's one book so far, *Nil Nil* (1993), slyly and
stylishly bears out, in a way, what he has given as a credo:
'technical considerations aside, bad poems generally try to
offer solutions, while good ones leave a little more fear, chaos,

wonder or mystery in the world than there was before'. His invented 'Aussemain', whose 'Pensées' yield him epigraphs, is a Borgesian figure, most obviously in 'The Alexandrian Library' ('Nothing is ever lost; things only become irretrievable'), an inventive and often very funny excursion into the detritus of literature and of memory. In the title-poem, the method is more like John Ashbery, full of whimsical narration and equally whimsical signals to the reader:

> the engine plopped out
> and would not re-engage, sending him silently
> twirling away like an ash-key,
> his attempt to bail out only partly successful,
> yesterday having been April the 1st –
> the ripcord unleashing a flurry of socks
> like a sackful of doves rendered up to the heavens
> in private irenicon. He caught up with the plane
> on the ground, just at the instant the tank blew
> and made nothing of him, save for his fillings,
> his tackets, his lucky half-crown and his gallstone,
> now anchored between the steel bars of a stank
> that looks to be biting the bullet on this one.

> *In short, this is where you get off, reader;*
> *I'll continue alone, on foot, in the failing light,*
> *following the trail as it steadily fades*
> *into road repairs, birdsong, the weather, nirvana,*
> *the plot thinning down to a point so refined*
> *not even the angels could dance on it. Goodbye.*

Just as teasing and even more in the uniform of the dandy, the poems of Michael Donaghy (*Shibboleth*, 1988, and *Errata*, 1993) are quirky and elegant, and they have the advantage of knowing when to stop: one debility of what might be called 'the new playfulness', it seems to me, is the Ashberyan one of allowing the joke or the whimsy or the supercilious surmise to run on too long a lead. Donaghy can be crisp:

One didn't know the name of Tarzan's monkey.
Another couldn't strip the cellophane
From a GI's pack of cigarettes.
By such minutiae were the infiltrators detected.

By the second week of battle
We'd become obsessed with trivia.
At a sentry point, at midnight, in the rain,
An ignorance of baseball could be lethal.

The morning of the first snowfall, I was shaving,
Staring into a mirror nailed to a tree,
Intoning the Christian names of the Andrews Sisters.
'Maxine, Laverne, Patty.'

('Shibboleth')★

There are two kinds of people in the world.
Roughly. First there are the kind who say
'There are two kinds of people in the world'
And then there's those who don't.

Me, I live smack on the borderline,
Where the road ends with towers and searchlights,
And we're kept awake all night by the creak of the barrier
Rising and falling like Occam's razor.

('Meridian')★

Donaghy is an American who has lived for some years in England: he partly earns his living working with Irish musicians, and America, Ireland and music all find a place in his poems.

The most consistently inventive and entertaining of all these seriously playful and deliberately disarming 'New Generation' poets, for me, is Ian Duhig, in whose *The Bradford Count* (1991) wry charm and riddling anecdotes alternate:

> According to Dineen, a Gael unsurpassed
> in lexicographical enterprise, the Irish
> for moon means 'the white circle in a slice
> of half-boiled potato or turnip'. A star
> is the mark on the forehead of a beast
> and the sun is the bottom of a lake, or well.
>
> Well, if I say to you your face
> is like a slice of half-boiled turnip,
> your hair is the colour of a lake's bottom
> and at the centre of each of your eyes
> is the mark of the beast, it is because
> I want to love you properly, according to Dineen.
>
> ('From the Irish')★
>
> Brethren, I know many of you have come here today
> because your Chief has promised any non-attender
> that he will stake them out, drive tent-pegs through his anus
> and sell his wives and children to the Portuguese.
> As far as possible, I want you to put that from your minds.
> Today, I want to talk to you about the Christian God.
>
> In many respects, our Christian God is not like your God.
> His name, for example, is not also our word for rain.
> Neither does it have for us the connotation 'sexual
>   intercourse'.
> And although I call Him 'holy' (we call Him 'Him' not 'It',

even though we know He is not a man and certainly not a
  woman)
I do not mean, as you do, that He is fat like a healthy cow.

Let me make this clear. When I say 'God is good, God is
  everywhere',
it is not because he is exceptionally fat. 'God loves you'
does not mean what warriors do to spear-carriers on
  campaign.
It means He feels for you like your mother or your father –
yes I know Chuma loved a son he bought like warriors
love spear carriers on campaign – that's *Sin* and it comes later.

From today, I want you to remember just three simple things:
our God is different from your God, our God is better than
  your God
and my wife doesn't like it when you watch her go to the
  toilet.
Grasp them and you have grasped the fundamentals of
  salvation.
Baptisms start at sundown but before then, as arranged,
how to strip, clean, and re-sight a bolt-action Martini-Henry.

('Fundamentals')★

All these poets mentioned so far in this section – Armitage,
Maxwell, Paterson, Donaghy, Duhig – for all the differences
between them are not only male (which isn't an important
point) but in their various ways *ludic* – a current buzz-word in
literary criticism, which finds respectable ancestry in Auden's
later work, in the poetry and fiction of Borges, and in Ashbery.
Carol Ann Duffy seems to owe little or nothing to such
examples. She first made her mark in the early 1980s with a
number of poems which were monologues, spoken by invented
characters (both female and male) who leapt into life through
the sheer force of the personality behind them. In other words,

Duffy effaced herself by finding dramatic ways of finding a range of voices – harsh, coarse, tender, puzzled – which were always dramatic, not drawing attention to the inventive poet she was and is. *Standing Female Nude* (1985), her first book, immediately thrust her forward. It contains such poems as 'Comprehensive', a dense but also plain interweaving of seven different voices – African, Pakistani, boys, girls, both hard-faced and soft English – which effectively speaks not just for a school but for a society; 'Words of Absolution', which wanders in and out of the consciousness of a ninety-year-old Catholic woman; 'You Jane', the voice of a toughly insensitive working–class husband; the title-poem, a nineteenth-century Paris artist's model; the suave evasions of a Nazi survivor, in 'What Price?'

In further books, Duffy has gone on extending her range of voices and manners: hectoring, seductive, desolate, almost destroyed, coarsely raucous, with a marvellous ear for speech, often rammed home in very short sentences, or sometimes in single punctuated words – this last an effective trick, but also close to a parodiable mannerism, though Duffy isn't easy to parody:

Turnover. Profit. Readies. Cash. Loot. Dough. Income. Stash.
Dosh. Bread. Finance. Brass. I give my tongue over
to money; the taste of warm rust in a chipped mug
of tap-water. Drink some yourself. Consider
an Indian man in Delhi, Salaamat the *niyariwallah*,
who squats by an open drain for hours, sifting shit
for the price of a chapati. More than that. His hands
in crumbling gloves of crap pray at the drains
for the pearls in slime his grandfather swore he found.

('Making Money')

There are also love poems of intense sensuality, loss, brisk cynicism, nostalgia – unflinching and flinching – which often take great risks (and there is an unexpected link here with

James Fenton's love poems in *Out of Danger*), speaking directly
and nakedly:

> The loveless men and homeless boys are out there and
>   angry.
> Nightly people end their lives in the shortcut.
> Walk in the light, steadily hurry towards me.
> Safety, safely, safe home.   (Who loves you?)
> Safety, safely, safe home.
>
>
>   ('Who Loves You?')

Duffy's most recent individual book, *Mean Time* (1993), is
recognisably by the same poet, but is more directly personal,
in its calling-up of memories of childhood, adolescence, the
memory of earlier loves as one grows older. She still plays
with voices – not her own voice – which can be absurd,
poignant, and male ('The Captain of the 1964 *Top of the Form*
Team') and chillingly cynical ('The Biographer'); but she is
now more willing to be listened to for herself and not just
her extraordinary mimetic skills. And her confidence in all
this now evidently means that she can take on the risk (or so
it sometimes seems, in these late post-modernist years of the
twentieth-century) of writing with proverbially old-fashioned
formality:

> Some days, although we cannot pray, a prayer
> utters itself. So, a woman will lift
> her head from the sieve of her hands and stare
> at the minims sung by a tree, a sudden gift.
>
> Some nights, although we are faithless, the truth
> enters our hearts, that small familiar pain;
> then a man will stand stock-still, hearing his youth
> in the distant Latin chanting of a train.

Pray for us now. Grade 1 piano scales
console the lodger looking out across
a Midlands town. Then dusk, and someone calls
a child's name as though they named their loss.

Darkness outside. Inside, the radio's prayer –
Rockall. Malin. Dogger. Finisterre.

('Prayer')*

Carol Ann Duffy has written of *Mean Time* that it 'tries to
record the brief words we hear and speak under the clock. In
that effort, at least, I hope it is optimistic.' In her case, they
seem words both true and brave, as we approach the end of the
century.

19

'The Poetry Business'

The economic recessions and stringencies in Britain in the 1980s and 1990s have naturally affected 'the poetry business', but not so much poets and the poems they write: poets are not easily crushed by economics, however depressed the condition of publishers, the exigencies of bookselling, or the fluctuating fortunes of journals, broadcasting, arts councils, funding bodies, and the like. Poets expect little from such sources, now or in the past. Nevertheless, in looking through earlier versions of this survey, stretching back to 1973, I have been struck by a number of socio-economic changes, changes which do mark out differences between the poetry business then and now.

There have been changes in attitudes, status and funding in such bodies as the Arts Council of England (formerly of Great Britain), the various regional arts boards (formerly councils), the Poetry Society, the Poetry Book Society, and – increasingly – the private sector. The Arts Council, following a Thatcherite and post-Thatcherite pattern one sees elsewhere in Britain, went in first for 'devolution' (that is, ostensibly, giving up central funding of the arts, including poetry, and appearing to allow regional bodies to take over such functions) and more recently for 'diversification' (that is, encouraging minorities and special groups – everything from racial minorities to women, gays, lesbians, the handicapped, the old, 'the disadvantaged'). What this often meant in practice was that 'devolution' produced less money, and that 'diversification' gave sporadic token help to the supposedly deprived without doing anything much about anyone else. More recently, the Arts Council Literature Department has received some increases and has steadied its nerve, to some extent.

In different ways, both the Poetry Society and the Poetry Book Society have been affected by such policy changes. The Poetry Society was in financial disarray for some years, moved to new and shrunken premises, and no longer seems to have the means or machinery to organise nationwide readings and visits by poets in the way it very actively did at one time with its National Poetry Secretariat. The formerly flourishing 'Poets in Schools' scheme, though it still exists, is less active than it was. Resident posts (so-called 'poets-in-residence') here and there function and/or flourish in schools, colleges, libraries, prisons, and also in a handful of universities, in which they are sometimes seen to be tolerated rather than encouraged. The Poetry Book Society, on the other hand, which has gone through many changes and vicissitudes since it was founded by T.S. Eliot and others in 1954, has actually increased its membership, and its distribution of books and members is now over twice as large as it was – closer to 2000 than 1000.

Such things as poetry prizes have benefited from injections of money from commerce: Sotheby's the art-dealers, *The Observer* newspaper, and W.H. Smith's the newsagents were fairly early in the field, but there are also a variety of newspapers, banks, and even individuals, who sporadically help with this or that prize – the T.S. Eliot Memorial Prize, the Forward Poetry Prize (each giving £10,000 to the overall winner), and others. National poetry competitions such as the Arvon and the National Poetry Competition still continue, drawing in thousands of entrants anonymously each year. And there are many others, listed in the Poetry Society's magazine, *Poetry Review*.

Among journals and magazines, the *Listener* finally collapsed after sixty years, and *Encounter* after over thirty years: both had been notable as places in which new poems were published and new books of poetry reviewed. Book publishers went through many changes of fortune, with many poetry lists shrunk or disappearing. Such specialist houses as Bloodaxe (based in Newcastle) and Carcanet (based in Manchester) seem as productive as ever, in both cases partly subsidised by private and public patrons. The main commercial publishers of poetry are now Faber & Faber (as for so long), Chatto & Windus (much diminished), Cape and Oxford University Press. Penguin Books, which successfully ran its *Penguin Modern Poets* between 1962 and 1979, after a lapse of years re-launched the series in 1995. There is still a range of 'little' magazines specialising in poetry: as I write, the leaders are *Poetry Review* (mentioned above) and *PN Review*, from Carcanet. Among the weeklies, fortnightlies and monthlies, *The Times Literary Supplement, New Statesman &*

Society, the *London Magazine*, and the *London Review of Books* are still hospitable to new poems; and some of the national Sundays occasionally allow some space – *The Sunday Times, The Observer, The Independent on Sunday*. The daily *Independent* has followed a curious policy of publishing each day a new poem, by the good, the bad, and the indifferent, genially paying for none of them.

In broadcasting, there has been a shift in recent years both in emphasis and in networks. The BBC's Radio 4, largely given to speech, and aiming at the intelligent but non-literary middlebrow audience, has become more generous to poetry, with the weekly request programme 'Poetry Please!' usually including some contemporary poetry and often a living poet, and with other programmes putting a particular emphasis on new poetry. On the other hand, Radio 3, which ancestrally (and as the Third Programme, founded soon after the Second World War) gave regular and ample space to new poetry, including the long-lived series 'The Poet's Voice' and 'Poetry Now' from the 1950s to the 1980s, has become almost exclusively a serious music programme, and the appearance of poetry is occasional and often archival rather than new, with no opportunity given – as in the former 'magazine' programmes – for the emergent poet to appear alongside established living poets. This seems a missed opportunity, when one remembers that such very different poets as Christopher Logue, Philip Larkin, Ted Hughes, James Fenton, Wendy Cope and Peter Reading helped to establish their early reputations by appearing in such miscellaneous or 'magazine' poetry programmes on the Third Programme and Radio 3.

BBC Radio 1, almost entirely transmitting pop music, had a surprising brief foray into poetry in 1994, when twenty young poets had their work broadcast as part of a cleverly promoted campaign. (Meanwhile Radio 5, which formerly attempted to give some space to poetry of a more popular sort, has become a news programme.) Altogether, there seems little sense of purpose or consistency in what has been going on. The various television networks, both BBC and commercial, have never known quite how to deal with poetry: brave tries have been made, there have been some notable triumphs (such as Tony Harrison's *V*, mentioned earlier in this survey), but in general there is no sign of a change in this blankness.

Nevertheless, there is a continuing buzz in the press that these are heady days for poetry. The 'Poems on the

Underground' scheme, whereby selected poems (old and new) are displayed among the advertisements on London Underground trains, has certainly had some impact, its accompanying anthologies selling very well, and the scheme spreading to other cities, and indeed other countries. The poet and critic Blake Morrison has chasteningly put such hype in context:

> Just so long as we're clear what this means, though – that poetry in this country is an amateur activity, the art of a band of enthusiasts (a bit like train-spotters), whose chief readers are not the customers of Waterstone's [the chain of booksellers] but each other. It will take a lot more than a single promotion to alter that.

Select Bibliography

The poet's birth-date follows the name.

When a poet has produced a comprehensive volume of Collected (or sometimes Selected) Poems, details of earlier volumes have been on the whole omitted.

ABSE, Dannie (1923–)
White Coat, Purple Coat: Collected Poems 1948–1988 (Hutchinson, 1989). *Remembrance of Crimes Past* (Hutchinson, 1990). *On the Evening Road* (Hutchinson, 1994). *Selected Poems* (Penguin, 1994).

ADCOCK, Fleur (1934–)
The Incident Book (OUP, 1986). *Time Zones* (OUP, 1991). *Selected Poems* (OUP, 1991).

ALVAREZ, A. (1929–)
Autumn to Autumn: Selected Poems 1953–1976 (Macmillan, 1978).

ALVI, Moniza (1954–)
The Country at my Shoulder (OUP, 1993).

AMIS, Kingsley (1922–)
Collected Poems 1944–1979 (Hutchinson, 1979).

ARMITAGE, Simon (1963–)
Zoom! (Bloodaxe, 1989). *Xanadu* (Bloodaxe, 1992). *Kid* (Faber, 1992). *Book of Matches* (Faber, 1993).

AUDEN, W.H. (1907–73)
Collected Poems (Faber, 1991).

BARKER, George (1913–91)
Collected Poems (Faber, 1987). *Street Ballads* (Faber, 1992).

BETJEMAN, John (1906–84)
Collected Poems (Murray, 1958; rev. 1979). *Summoned by Bells* (Murray, 1960). *Uncollected Poems* (Murray, 1982).

BHATT, Sujata (1956–)
Brunizem (Carcanet, 1988). *Monkey Shadows* (Carcanet, 1991). *The Stinking Rose* (Carcanet, 1995).

BROCK, Edwin (1927–)
Five Ways to Kill a Man: New and Selected Poems (Enitharmon Press, 1990).

BROWN, George Mackay (1921–)
Selected Poems 1954–1983 (Murray, 1991).

BROWNJOHN, Alan (1931–)
Collected Poems 1952–1988 (Hutchinson, 1988). *The Observation Car* (Hutchinson, 1990). *In the Cruel Arcade* (Sinclair-Stevenson, 1994).

BUNTING, Basil (1900–85)
The Complete Poems (OUP, 1994).

CAUSLEY, Charles (1917–)
Collected Poems 1951–92
(Macmillan, 1992).

CLARKE, Gillian (1937–)
Selected Poems (Carcanet, 1985).
Letting in the Rumour (Carcanet,
1989). *The King of Britain's
Daughter* (Carcanet, 1993).

CONQUEST, Robert (1917–)
New and Collected Poems
(Hutchinson, 1988).

COPE, Wendy (1945–)
Making Cocoa for Kingsley Amis
(Faber, 1986). *Serious Concerns*
(Faber, 1991).

CRAWFORD, Robert (1959–)
A Scottish Assembly (Chatto &
Windus, 1990). *Talkies* (Chatto &
Windus, 1992).

DABYDEEN, David (1956–)
Turner: New and Selected Poems
(Cape, 1994).

D'AGUIAR, Fred (1960–)
Airy Hall (Chatto & Windus,
1989). *British Subjects* (Bloodaxe,
1993).

DAVIE, Donald (1922–)
Collected Poems (Carcanet, 1990).

DAY LEWIS, C. (1904–72)
The Complete Poems (Sinclair-
Stevenson, 1992).

DONAGHY, Michael (1954–)
Shibboleth (OUP, 1988). *Errata*
(OUP, 1993).

DOWNIE, Freda (1929–93)
Collected Poems (Bloodaxe, 1995).

DUFFY, Carol Ann (1955–)
Selected Poems (Penguin Books,
1994).

DUHIG, Ian (1954–)
The Bradford Count (Bloodaxe,
1991). *The Mersey Goldfish*
(Bloodaxe, 1995).

DUNN, Douglas (1942–)
Selected Poems 1964–1983 (Faber,
1986). *Northlight* (Faber, 1988).
Dante's Drum-kit (Faber, 1993).

DURCAN, Paul (1944–)
*A Snail in My Prime: New and
Selected Poems* (Harvill/Blackstaff
Press, 1993).

DURRELL, Lawrence (1912–91)
Collected Poems 1931–1974 (Faber,
1980).

ELIOT, T.S. (1888–1965)
The Complete Poems and Plays
(Faber, 1969).

ELLIOT, Alistair (1932–)
My Country: Collected Poems
(Carcanet, 1989). *Turning the
Stones* (Carcanet, 1993).

EMPSON, William (1906–84)
Collected Poems (Chatto & Windus, 1955)

ENRIGHT, D.J. (1920–)
Collected Poems (OUP, 1987).
Under the Circumstances (OUP, 1991). *Old Men and Comets* (OUP, 1993).

EWART, Gavin (1916–)
The Collected Ewart 1933–1980 (Hutchinson 1980).
Collected Poems 1980–1990 (Hutchinson, 1991). *85 Poems* (Hutchinson, 1993).

FAINLIGHT, Ruth (1931–)
Selected Poems (Hutchinson, 1987).
Selected Poems (Sinclair-Stevenson, 1995).

FANTHORPE, U.A. (1929–)
Selected Poems (Penguin, 1989).
Neck-Verse (Peterloo, 1992).

FEAVER, Vicki (1943–)
Close Relatives (Secker & Warburg, 1981). *The Handless Maiden* (Cape, 1994).

FEINSTEIN, Elaine (1930–)
Selected Poems (Carcanet, 1994).

FENTON, James (1949–)
The Memory of War and Children in Exile: Poems 1968–1983 (Penguin, 1983). *Out of Danger* (Penguin, 1993).

FISHER, Roy (1930–)
Poems 1955–1987 (OUP, 1988).
Birmingham River (OUP, 1994).

FORD, Mark (1962–)
Landlocked (Chatto & Windus, 1992).

FULLER, John (1937–)
Selected Poems 1954–1982 (Secker & Warburg, 1985). *The Grey Among the Green* (Chatto & Windus, 1988). *The Mechanical Body* (Chatto & Windus, 1991).

FULLER, Roy (1912–91)
New and Collected Poems 1934–84 (Secker & Warburg, 1985).
Subsequent to Summer (Salamander Press, 1985). *Consolations* (Secker & Warburg, 1987). *Available for Dreams* (Collins Harvill, 1989). *Last Poems* (Sinclair-Stevenson, 1993).

GARIOCH, Robert (1909–80)
Complete Poetical Works (Macdonald, 1983).

GARRETT, Elizabeth (1958–)
The Rule of Three (Bloodaxe, 1991).

GASCOYNE, David (1916–)
Collected Poems (OUP, 1988).

GRAHAM, W.S. (1918–86)
Collected Poems 1942–1977 (Faber, 1979).

GRAVES, Robert (1895–1985)
Collected Poems (Cassell, 1992).

GREENLAW, Lavinia (1962–)
Night Photographs (Faber, 1993).

GRIGSON, Geoffrey (1905–85)
Collected Poems 1924–1962
(Phoenix House, 1963). *The
Cornish Dancer* (Secker &
Warburg, 1982). *Collected Poems
1963–80* (Allison & Busby,
1982). *Montaigne's Tower* (Secker
& Warburg, 1984). *Persephone's
Flowers* (Secker & Warburg, 1986).

GUNN, Thom (1929–)
Collected Poems (Faber, 1993).

HAMBURGER, Michael (1924–)
Collected Poems 1941–1994 (Anvil,
1994).

HAMILTON, Ian (1938–)
Fifty Poems (Faber, 1988).

HARRISON, Tony (1937–)
Selected Poems (Viking, 1989). *V*
(Bloodaxe, 1989). *A Cold Coming*
(Bloodaxe, 1991). *The Gaze of the
Gorgon* (Bloodaxe, 1992).

HARSENT, David (1942–)
Selected Poems (OUP, 1989). *News
from the Front* (OUP, 1993).

HEANEY, Seamus (1939–)
Selected Poems 1965–1975 (Faber,
1980). *Field Work* (Faber, 1979).
Station Island (Faber, 1984). *The*

Haw Lantern (Faber, 1987). *Seeing
Things* (Faber, 1991).

HEATH-STUBBS, John (1918–)
Collected Poems 1943–1987
(Carcanet, 1988). *Sweetapple Earth*
(Carcanet, 1993).

HEGLEY, John (1953–)
Glad to Wear Glasses (Deutsch,
1990). *Can I Come Down Now
Dad?* (Methuen, 1991). *Five Sugars
Please* (Methuen, 1993). *These were
Your Father's* (Methuen, 1994).

HENRI, Adrian (1932–)
Collected Poems 1967–1985 (Allison
& Busby, 1986). *Wish You Were
Here* (Cape, 1990). *Not Fade Away*
(Bloodaxe, 1994).

HERBERT, W.N. (1961–)
Forked Tongue (Bloodaxe, 1994).

HILL, Geoffrey (1932–)
Collected Poems (Deutsch, 1985).

HOBSBAUM, Philip (1932–)
The Place's Fault (Macmillan,
1964). *In Retreat* (Macmillan,
1966). *Coming Out Fighting*
(Macmillan, 1969). *Women and
Animals* (Macmillan, 1972).

HOFMANN, Michael (1957–)
Nights in the Iron Hotel (Faber,
1983). *Acrimony* (Faber, 1986).
Corona, Corona (Faber, 1993).

HOLBROOK, David (1923–)
Selected Poems 1961–1978 (Anvil
Press, 1980).

HOROVITZ, Michael (1935–)
*Wordsounds and Sightlines: New and
Selected Poems* (Sinclair-Stevenson,
1994).

HUGHES, Glyn (1935–)
*Best of Neighbours: New and
Selected Poems* (Ceolfrith, 1979).

HUGHES, Ted (1930–)
Crow (Faber, 1970).
New Selected Poems 1957–1994
(Faber, 1995).

HULSE, Michael (1955–)
Knowing and Forgetting (Secker
& Warburg, 1981). *Propaganda*
(Secker & Warburg, 1985). *Eating
Strawberries in the Necropolis*
(Harvill, 1991). *Mother of Battles*
(Littlewood Arc, 1991).

IMLAH, Mick (1956–)
Birthmarks (Chatto & Windus,
1988).

JAMIE, Kathleen (1962–)
The Way We Live (Bloodaxe,
1987). *The Queen of Sheba*
(Bloodaxe, 1994).

JAMES, Clive (1939–)
Other Passports: Poems 1958–1985
(Cape, 1986).

JENKINS, Alan (1955–)
In the Hot-House (Chatto &
Windus, 1988). *Greenheart* (Chatto

& Windus, 1990). *Harm* (Chatto &
Windus, 1994).

JENNINGS, Elizabeth (1926–)
Growing Points (Carcanet, 1975).
Collected Poems 1953–1985
(Carcanet, 1986). *Tributes*
(Carcanet, 1989). *Times and
Seasons* (Carcanet, 1992). *Familiar
Spirits* (Carcanet, 1994).

JOHNSON, Adam (1965–93)
The Playground Bell (Carcanet,
1994).

JONES, David (1895–1974)
In Parenthesis (Faber, 1937). *The
Anathemata* (Faber, 1952). *The
Tribune's Visitation* (Fulcrum Press,
1969). *The Sleeping Lord and Other
Fragments* (Agenda, 1974). *The
Kensington Mass* (Agenda, 1975).
*The Roman Quarry and Other
Sequences* (University of Wales
Press, 1981).

JOSEPH, Jenny (1932–)
Selected Poems (Bloodaxe, 1992).

KAVANAGH, P.J. (1931–)
Collected Poems (Carcanet, 1992).

KAY, Jackie (1961–)
The Adoption Papers (Bloodaxe,
1991). *Other Lovers* (Bloodaxe,
1993).

KINSELLA, Thomas (1928–)
Selected Poems 1956–1973 (Dolmen
Press, 1980).

LARKIN, Philip (1922–85)
Collected Poems (Marvell
Press/Faber, 1988).

LEONARD, Tom (1944–)
*Intimate Voices: Selected Work
1965–83* (Galloping Dog Press,
1984). *Situations Theoretical and
Contemporary* (Galloping Dog
Press, 1986).

LERNER, Laurence (1925–)
Selected Poems (Secker & Warburg,
1984). *Chapter and Verse* (Secker
& Warburg, 1984). *Rembrandt's
Mirror* (Secker & Warburg, 1987).

LOCHHEAD, Liz (1947–)
Bagpipe Muzak (Penguin, 1991).

LOGUE, Christopher (1926–)
Ode to the Dodo: Poems 1953–1978
(Cape, 1981). *War Music* (Cape,
1981). *Kings* (Cape, 1991). *The
Husbands* (Faber, 1994).

LONGLEY, Michael (1939–)
Poems 1963–1983 (Salamander
Press, 1985), *Gorse Fires* (Secker
& Warburg, 1991). *Ghost Orchid*
(Cape, 1995).

LUCIE-SMITH, Edward (1993–)
An Exploded View. Poems 1968–72
(Gollamez, 1973).
A Tropical Childhood (OUP,
1961). *Confessions and Histories*
(OUP, 1964). *Towards Silence*
(OUP, 1968). *The Well-Wishers*
(OUP, 1974).

MacBETH, George (1932–92)
Collected Poems 1958–1982
(Hutchinson, 1989). *Anatomy

of a Divorce* (Hutchinson, 1988).
Trespassing (Hutchinson, 1991).
The Patient (Hutchinson, 1992).

MacCAIG, Norman (1910–)
Collected Poems (Chatto & Windus,
1993).

MacDIARMID, Hugh (1892–1978)
The Complete Poems (Carcanet,
1995).

McGOUGH, Roger (1937–)
*Blazing Fruit: Selected Poems
1967–87* (Penguin, 1990). *You at
the Back: Selected Poems 1967–87,
vol. 2* (Cape, 1991).

McGUCKIAN, Medbh (1950–)
The Flower Master (OUP, 1982).
Venus and the Rain (OUP, 1984).
On Ballycastle Beach (OUP, 1988).
Marconi's Cottage (Bloodaxe,
1992).

MACKINNON, Lachlan (1956–)
Monterey Cypress (Chatto &
Windus, 1988). *The Coast of
Bohemia* (Chatto & Windus, 1991).

MacNEICE, Louis (1907–63)
Collected Poems (Faber, 1966).

MAGUIRE, Sarah (1957–)
Spilt Milk (Secker & Warburg,
1991).

MAHON, Derek (1941–)
Selected Poems (Viking 1991).

MAXWELL, Glyn (1962–)
Tale of the Mayor's Son (Bloodaxe, 1990). *Out of the Rain* (Bloodaxe, 1992). *Rest for the Wicked* (Bloodaxe, 1995).

MITCHELL, Adrian (1932–)
For Beauty Douglas: Collected Poems 1953–1979 (Allison & Busby, 1982). *On the Beach at Cambridge* (Allison & Busby, 1984). *Love Songs of World War Three* (Allison & Busby, 1989). *Adrian Mitchell's Greatest Hits* (Bloodaxe, 1991).

MITCHELL, Elma (1919–)
People Etcetera: Poems New and Selected (Peterloo, 1987).

MOLE, John (1941–)
Selected Poems (Sinclair-Stevenson, 1995).

MORGAN, Edwin (1920–)
Collected Poems (Carcanet, 1990). *Sweeping Out the Dark* (Carcanet, 1994).

MORGAN, Pete (1939–)
The Grey Mare Being the Better Steed (Secker & Warburg, 1973). *The Spring Collection* (Secker & Warburg, 1979). *A Winter Visitor* (Secker & Warburg, 1984).

MORRISON, Blake (1950–)
Dark Glasses (Chatto & Windus, 1984; rev. and enlarged, 1989). *The Ballad of the Yorkshire Ripper* (Chatto & Windus, 1987).

MOTION, Andrew (1952–)
Dangerous Play: Poems 1974–1984 (Salamander Press, 1984). *Natural Causes* (Chatto & Windus, 1987). *Love in a Life* (Faber, 1991). *The Price of Everything* (Faber, 1994).

MULDOON, Paul (1951–)
Why Brownlee Left (Faber, 1980). *Selected Poems 1968–1983* (Faber, 1986). *Meeting the British* (Faber, 1987). *Madoc* (Faber, 1990). *Shining Brow* (Faber, 1993). *The Annals of Chile* (Faber, 1994).

MURPHY, Richard (1927–)
New Selected Poems (Faber, 1989).

NICHOLS, Grace (1950–)
The Fat Black Woman's Poems (Virago, 1984). *Lazy Thoughts of a Lazy Woman* (Virago, 1989).

NICHOLSON, Norman (1914–87)
Collected Poems (Faber, 1994).

O'BRIEN, Sean (1952–)
The Indoor Park (Bloodaxe, 1983). *The Frighteners* (Bloodaxe, 1987). *HMS Glasshouse* (OUP, 1991).

ORMSBY, Frank (1947–)
A Store of Candles (OUP, 1977). *A Northern Spring* (Secker & Warburg, 1986).

PATERSON, Don (1963–)
Nil Nil (Faber, 1993).

PATTEN, Brian (1946–)
Growing Jack: Selected Poems (Unwin Hyman, 1990).

PAULIN, Tom (1949–)
Selected Poems 1972–1990 (Faber, 1993). *Walking a Line* (Faber, 1994).

PESKETT, William (1952–)
The Nightowl's Dissection (Secker & Warburg, 1975). *Survivors* (Secker & Warburg, 1980).

PITT-KETHLEY, Fiona (1954–)
Sky Ray Lolly (Chatto & Windus, 1986). *Private Parts* (Chatto & Windus, 1987). *The Perfect Man* (Abacus, 1989). *Dogs* (Sinclair-Stevenson, 1993).

PLATH, Sylvia (1932–63)
Collected Poems (Faber, 1981).

PLOMER, William (1903–73)
Collected Poems (Cape, 1973).

PORTER, Peter (1929–)
Collected Poems (OUP, 1983). *Fast Forward* (OUP, 1984). *The Automatic Oracle* (OUP, 1987). *Possible Worlds* (OUP, 1989). *The Chair of Babel* (OUP, 1992). *Millennial Fables* (OUP, 1994).

PRICE, Jonathan (1931–85)
Everything Must Go (Secker & Warburg, 1985).

RAINE, Craig (1944–)
The Onion, Memory (OUP, 1978). *A Martian Sends a Postcard Home* (OUP, 1979). *Rich* (Faber, 1984). *History: The Home Movie* (Penguin, 1994).

RAINE, Kathleen (1908–)
Collected Poems 1935–1980 (Allen & Unwin, 1981). *The Presence* (Golgonooza, 1987). *Living with Mystery* (Golgonooza, 1992).

READING, Peter (1946–)
Essential Reading (Secker & Warburg, 1986). *Stet* (Secker & Warburg, 1986). *Final Demands* (Secker & Warburg, 1988). *Perduta Gente* (Secker & Warburg, 1989). *Shitheads* (Squirrelprick, 1989). *3 in 1* (Chatto & Windus, 1992). *Evagatory* (Chatto & Windus, 1992). *Last Poems* (Chatto & Windus, 1994). *Collected Poems 1: Poems 1970–84* (Bloodaxe, 1995).

REDGROVE, Peter (1932–)
The Moon Disposes: Poems 1954–1987 (Penguin, 1989). *The First Earthquake* (Secker & Warburg, 1989). *Under the Reservoir* (Secker & Warburg, 1992). *My Father's Trapdoors* (Cape, 1994).

REEVES, James (1909–78)
Collected Poems 1929–1974 (Heinemann, 1974).

REID, Christopher (1950–)
Arcadia (OUP, 1979). *Pea Soup* (OUP, 1982). *Katerina Brac* (Faber, 1985). *In the Echoey Tunnel* (Faber, 1991).

RIDLER, Anne (1912–)
Collected Poems (Carcanet, 1994).

RUMENS, Carol (1943–)
Selected Poems (Chatto & Windus,
1987). *From Berlin to Heaven*
(Chatto & Windus, 1989).
*Thinking of Skins: New and Selected
Poems* (Bloodaxe, 1993).

SATYAMURTI, Carole (1939–)
Broken Moon (OUP, 1987).
Changing the Subject (OUP, 1990).
Striking Distance (OUP, 1994).

SCANNELL, Vernon (1922–)
Collected Poems 1950–1993 (Robson
Books, 1994).

SCOVELL, E.J. (1907–)
Collected Poems (Carcanet, 1988).

SCUPHAM, Peter (1933–)
Selected Poems (OUP, 1990).
Watching the Perseids (OUP, 1990).
The Ark (OUP, 1994).

SILKIN, Jon (1930–)
Selected Poems (Sinclair-Stevenson,
1994).

SIMMONS, James (1933–)
Selected Poems 1956–1986
(Bloodaxe, 1986).

SMITH, Iain Crichton (1928–)
Love Poems & Elegies (Gollancz,
1972).
Collected Poems (Carcanet, 1992).
Ends and Beginnings (Carcanet,
1994).

SMITH, Ken (1938–)
*The Poet Reclining: Selected Poems
1962–1980* (Bloodaxe, 1982).
Terra (Bloodaxe, 1986). *Wormwood*

(Bloodaxe, 1987). *Tender to the
Queen of Spain* (Bloodaxe, 1994).

SMITH, Stevie (1902–71)
Collected Poems (Penguin, 1989).

SMITH, Sydney Goodsir (1915–75)
Collected Poems 1941–75 (John
Calder, 1975).

SPENDER, Stephen (1909–95)
Collected Poems 1928–1985 (Faber,
1985). *Dolphins* (Faber, 1994).

STAINER, Pauline (1941–)
The Honeycomb (Bloodaxe, 1989).
Sighting the Slave Ship (Bloodaxe,
1992). *The Ice-Pilot Speaks*
(Bloodaxe, 1994).

STALLWORTHY, Jon (1935–)
*The Anzac Sonata: New and
Selected Poems* (Chatto & Windus,
1986).

SZIRTES, George (1948–)
The Slant Door (Secker &
Warburg, 1979). *November and
May* (Secker & Warburg, 1981).
Short Wave (Secker & Warburg,
1983). *The Photographer in Winter*
(Secker & Warburg, 1986). *Metro*
(OUP, 1988). *Bridge Passages*
(OUP, 1991). *Blind Field* (OUP,
1994).

THOMAS, D.M. (1935–)
*The Puberty Tree: New and Selected
Poems* (Bloodaxe, 1992).

THOMAS, R.S. (1913–   )
Collected Poems 1945–1990 (Dent,
1993).

THWAITE, Anthony (1930–   )
Poems 1953–1988 (Hutchinson,
1989). *The Dust of the World*
(Sinclair-Stevenson, 1994).

TOMLINSON, Charles (1927–   )
Collected Poems (OUP, 1987). *The
Return* (OUP, 1987). *Annunciations*
(OUP, 1989). *The Door in the
Wall* (OUP, 1992). *Jubilation*
(OUP, 1995).

TRIPP, John (1927–86)
Selected Poems (Seren, 1989).

WAIN, John (1925–94)
Poems 1949–1979 (Macmillan,
1981). *Open Country* (Hutchinson,
1987).

WALKER, Ted (1934–   )
Hands at a Live Fire: Selected Poems
(Secker & Warburg, 1987).

WHITWORTH, John (1945–   )
Unhistorical Fragments (Secker &
Warburg, 1980). *Poor Butterflies*
(Secker & Warburg, 1982).
Lovely Day for a Wedding (Secker
& Warburg, 1985). *Tennis and
Sex and Death* (Peterloo, 1989).
Landscape with Small Humans
(Peterloo, 1993).

WICKS, Susan (1947–   )
Singing Underwater (Faber, 1992).
Open Diagnosis (Faber, 1994).

WILLIAMS, Hugo (1942–   )
Selected Poems (OUP, 1989).
Self-Portrait with a Slide (OUP,
1990). *Dock Leaves* (Faber, 1994).

WRIGHT, Kit (1944–   )
Poems 1974–1983 (Hutchinson,
1988). *Short Afternoons*
(Hutchinson, 1989).

YOUNG, Andrew (1885–1971)
The Poetical Works (Secker &
Warburg, 1985).

ZEPHANIAH, Benjamin (1958–   )
The Dread Affair (Arena, 1985).
City Psalms (Bloodaxe, 1992).

Index